Presented to

_____

From

_____

Date

_____

Praise for "Step on a Crack"

"I'M STRUCK AND IMPRESSED BY Byrne's deadpan humor, piercing honesty, and the ability to tell a masterful story that could have easily turned out angry, bitter, or maudlin. She has a rare talent for storytelling. Her clear vision of what she endured growing up and how she doggedly worked to heal her inner self will inspire anyone who wonders how people survive in this zany world.

"Byrne's lovely literary voice, combined with the editorial talent of Michael Ransom, leaves you longing to read more."

—Kathleen Gleeson, co-author with Janusz Bardach of
Man is Wolf to Man: Surviving Stalin's Gulag and
Surviving Freedom: After the Gulag

"ALL OF US LEARN FROM challenges and obstacles. Some people have to go through the ordeal themselves, but some of us can learn from an example from someone else's life. Jill Byrne gives us a glimpse of her trials and tribulations. Through her experiences, we can begin to learn how to deal with our own."

—Jim Stovall, author of *The Ultimate Gift*

Step on a Crack,

OVERCOMING DEPRESSION: A MEMOIR

To Julia —
A friend extraordinar!
Thanks for supporting
this "swinging" endeavor!
Best,
Jill
5/5/13

Jill Byrne

with Michael Ransom

Step on a Crack
Overcoming Depression: A Memoir

Published by Wheatmark®
610 East Delano Street, Suite 104
Tucson, Arizona 85705 U.S.A.
www.wheatmark.com

International Standard Book Number: 978-1-60494-171-5
Library of Congress Control Number: 2008935252

Cover photo: Saturday morning at home with my mother and Janie Bumpers. We are standing in front of steps where I burned Janie's feet when she was a baby. Note: I'm wearing "rocket shoes," illustrating my lack of being grounded.

For
Porter, Maggie, and Gracie

In loving memory of
Frances, Clifford, and Beverly Byrne

Author's Note

T WAS NEVER MY INTENT to write anything, much less my memoir. However, when my significant bouts of depression ended abruptly and never returned over the test of time, with humble gratitude, I felt called to share my journey. My purpose was not to tell all, but to tell enough to encourage others in a similar situation.

Some names in this book were changed to protect privacy. While the events and conversations are essentially true, I compressed and streamlined some scenes and dialogue to aid narrative flow.

Contents

Acknowledgements

FIRST, A HEARTFELT THANKS TO my family. They listened without passing judgment while I wrote this book.

I am forever grateful for Mary Peitrini taking a moment to inspire me to begin a writing life on a Sunday afternoon in July 1993.

There are many people to thank for their support and encouragement over the years it took to get my story out and I'm regretfully confident I will leave out some names. If yours is one, I apologize. Most of those named stepped up as readers and all went out of their way to inquire and show they cared:

Paula Alfred, Tricia Arend, Phyllis Beam, Bob Bennett, Jim and Joanie Blevins, Barbara Booker, Barbara Brant, Louise Bray, Trigger Butler, Gil Broyles, Cathy and Ron Burden, Jeff Burns, Mary Coley, Tim Colwell, Margaret Ann Comito, Mark Darrah, Tami and Dave DeAngelis, Kate de Gutes, Barbara Detmer, Mieke Epps, Suzy Ewing, Helen Frady, Maggie Gilliland, Phil Graham, Mary and George Gurley, Janice Hall, Claire Harrah, Sue Hembree, Maret Herr, Lynn Hoke, Carolyn Hudson, Janie Huffman, Ruth Jacobs, Martin Keating, Martha Kilgore, Jackie King, Sharon Koons, Judy Kolz, Jean Lewis, Bond Love, Jocie and Wally Love, Lyn Lucas, Andrew Marshall, Janie McKinney, Judy Miller, Rod Nordstrom, the Oklabelles, Charlotte Parker, Shirley Powell, Suella Reagan, Margaret Reynolds, Paula Roberts, Jane Rosen, Armin Saeger, Blane Snodgrass, Phyllis Snyder, Janice Sprouse, Connie Stevens, Judy Stidham, Steve Syrja, the late Charles Tegeler, Ruth Thone, Jennifer Turner, Judy Waller, Carol Willis, Barbara Wollmershauser, Janet Word, Trigg and Bill Yerby, and my friends from Ada High.

Doris Booth, Peggy Fielding, Kate Gleeson, Cecile Goding, Annie Hawkins, Arlene Johnson, Judith Kitchen, Sandra Soli, Liz Abrams-

Morley, and Sara Kay Rupnik, all provided much needed professional guidance. Thank you. Special gratitude goes to editor, Tracy Robert who challenged me well beyond what I thought possible.

This book is in tribute to the late Gunda J. Palmer, my cheerleader extraordinaire.

And finally a special thank you to writer, Mike Ransom and his wife, Jeanine, who welcomed "a stranger needing help" into their home. His immediate willingness to take on this project was paramount in its conclusion. (Little did Mike know it would take an entire calendar year to just absorb my life!) The author was up front from day one that a Greater Power made this professional pairing. Mike's organizational skill and tireless gentle encouragement throughout engineered the process toward the cusp of completion.

Bless his heart. AJB

THE 2002 UNIVERSITY of Iowa Summer Writing Festival I attended not only convinced me I had some writing talent, but it also led me to Jill Byrne. She attended the Festival in 2003 looking for a writer to help her with her memoir. Jill attended Kate Gleeson's Writing Lives Workshop, which I had attended the year before. When Kate learned of Jill's search, she suggested me, and after a few weeks and several phone calls, Jill and I met to begin our work on *Step on a Crack*.

I commend Jill for trusting a "northerner" to help tell her story— one extremely poignant, personal, and painful in many places, yet so inspiring. In visiting her Ada, Oklahoma, hometown, in meeting many of her friends, co-workers, and therapists that appear in the book, and in countless hours of conversations between us, I came to appreciate Jill's patience and resolve. We shared many laughs, some tears, but never a discouraging word.

Today, more than five years after we began, I thank Jill for asking me to join her on her writing adventure. I feel I'm a better person for it. I also thank my wife, Jeanine, who accompanied me on several writing sessions with Jill in Tulsa, Oklahoma City, and Kansas City (conveniently located about half way between my home and Jill's).

Through my times with Jill, I gained an appreciation of her life's struggles. May she forever enjoy the normalcy she has attained. MJR

Nobody realizes that some people expend
tremendous energy merely to be normal.
Albert Camus

Introduction

I T WAS AN OVERCAST, EARLY spring Saturday afternoon in 2001 when I returned home from an infrequent massage. Only one message blinked on the machine.

"Jill, if you get this message before three o'clock, call me if you are still interested in going to that reading we talked about last year. Tina is in town for a few days, and she is doing a reading at four. Hope you get this. Talk to you later."

With minutes to spare, I reached Jennifer in time for her to swing by and pick me up.

She said, "The reading is at the EconoLodge out on Garnett Road, so, while we're riding, be thinking of a question you want to ask."

Jennifer sped along down a street, toward an area unfamiliar to me. We exchanged little conversation. We were both busy with our own thoughts; mine were sandwiched inside a spirit of adventure.

At the motel, I held my breath when I encountered that musty smell of stale cigarette smoke that had been left there long before the newly posted "No Smoking" signs.

I told myself, "Breathe through your mouth. Do not be deterred."

The placards in the lobby directed us down a hall, where we stopped at a table to pay for admission. We were given a slip of paper and pen and encouraged to hurry to Room 122 and write down a question because Tina would soon begin.

As is often the case, up-front seating was all that was left. Jennifer was pleased, as she preferred the front row. I, on the other hand, generally gravitate to the back, which was not an option today. I glanced around to the twenty-five or thirty others filling the room. I was somewhat grateful that I saw no familiar faces.

I wrote my question: should I really try to write a book?

Then we were told to fold the paper and hold it next to our hearts until Chuck came by to pick it up.

Once all questions were collected, Tina entered the room and was immediately blindfolded. Two additional types of blindfolds were also applied. She spoke briefly before singing Alabama's "Angels Among Us." She told us that Teensie was the name of her angel who helped her obtain contact with the other side. Then Chuck led her to the table with the tray of questions.

Her process of selecting each question was so similar to Johnny Carson's "Carnack the Magnificent" shtick that I had to exert an effort to suppress my giggles. One by one, Tina blindly asked if someone in the room wanted information from Kathy, Mary Sue, or Jim.

The questions included those such as:

- Is Danny the right man for me?
- Is my mother still in pain?
- Should I find another job?

While all were good questions with seemingly satisfying answers, after the first dozen, I began to feel doubtful whether my question would gain a response.

Then Tina said, "Does anyone know Taylor?"

The room was silent. When no one responded, I finally offered that Beverly Taylor was my sister's married name. Beverly had died in 1999.

Tina cleared her throat and said, "I don't understand what Taylor is trying to tell me, but here goes. First, there is a strong aura around your right hand, suggesting you are going to be doing a lot of writing. Taylor says it is okay to tell the story and you will be able to help more people than you will ever know."

I was blown away. The story that my sister encouraged me to tell involves my lifelong struggle with depression, of which I was cured over ten years ago while attending the Hoffman Quadrinity Process. Though extremely difficult to remove that psychiatric gum off one's shoe, I proved it could be done.

I don't remember the rest of the reading or how long it lasted, but, by the time Jennifer and I reached the car, I knew this Oklahoma girl would give it her best because her sister believed she could.

This is my story.

A Foretaste of Things to Come

1972

I T TOOK ME A LONG time to recover from my mother's attitude, which was something that started years before I was born. I was up against it for most of my life and hers.

Ellen Bumpers, my family's next-door neighbor, once told me, "I always thought you might end up in a mental institution."

She didn't say it to be mean. She had been an across-the-fence observer for much of my childhood. She feared I had suffered enough subtle neglect at an impressionable age that it could catch up with me later. She was right. It did.

Pushing almost one hundred pounds, I hovered near the medication window with nine or ten other psychiatric patients milling around after breakfast. When my name was called, I stepped up and accepted the paper nut cup, so aptly named, thrust toward me. Counting six various pills of who knows what, I got them down without incident. As I turned away from the window, I reached for the wall as the world turned by. I focused on the coolness from the wall tiles on my back and slid down. It was my twenty-sixth birthday, and I guess I missed it.

"Could you sit up and try to listen?" the therapist asked.

"What does he think I am doing?" I thought. I shifted to wrap my arms around my legs and rested my chin between my kneecaps.

"I'll try," I said. "It would help if you speak slower. For some reason, I can't listen as fast as you are talking."

I didn't remember the name of this therapist, but I was pretty sure I saw him in an office off the day room. Maybe it was yesterday. He seemed then to be making an effort to establish rapport, but it wasn't worth the trouble for me to meet him halfway. I only wanted to talk to Dr. Kravitz. They said it wasn't possible.

Now this doctor was sitting by my bed here in the ward. Only three other patients were assigned to the six-bed unit. Except for the two of us, the room was empty. They were probably in group.

"Why am I not in group?" I asked.

"You must not remember," he replied. "When meds were dispensed after breakfast, you didn't make it three steps before sliding down the wall. Calvin carried you to bed. And that's just it, Jill. You came in here almost a week ago in a near-catatonic state, and you have made virtually no progress in that time. The committee has decided you need long-term residential care, and it is now imperative we notify your family, whether you like it or not. Sign here. A social worker will give them a call."

"No," I answered.

Everything about this place was beige or gray, myself included. It was January, but I wouldn't know it on the psych ward. The heat blowing through the vents was so dry that I burst a blood vessel in my nose while brushing my teeth.

"Was it yesterday?" I thought.

A tech was assigned to accompany me through a tunnel system to a doctor's office in the medical building. An unfamiliar doctor cauterized my nose, and the tech walked me back to the ward. The last thing I remembered today was how cool the tile wall felt on my back.

The ping-pong table was in the hall to the left of our door. If I had an ounce of energy, I could have probably given David, the night shift psych tech, a better game than he would expect. The best I could do now was keep the ball in play.

On the other side of the wall from my bed was the room where electroshock treatments were administered. Listening to that process was enough to cure me of considering such a violent option.

My resolve to keep my mental health issues and my mother's presence separate overrode all other decisions. Not only was I released from the hospital with the firm admonition of "You will be back," but I was fully armed with a month's supply of Thorazine to tide me over.

Before Me, Family of Three

Before 1946

ADA, OKLAHOMA, IS SITUATED SOME ninety miles from Oklahoma City. In 1946, when I was born, Ada's fifteen thousand citizens considered themselves to be off the beaten path. Those who came to town intended to do so. Few were just passing through. Ada sported a four-year teacher's college, East Central, and enjoyed the cultural opportunities that accompanied a college town. With at least three movie houses and the Aldridge and Juliana hotels, downtown Ada bustled with activity. The announcement of my birth appeared on the sports page of the *Evening News* in a column called "Charley's Chatter":

> *It may not be a sports event, and it may not exactly belong on this page, but this column is proud to announce the birth of a daughter to Mr. and Mrs. Clifford Byrne. Ann Jill Byrne, as she will be called for the remainder of her life, was born at 9:05 PM Saturday (January 12), making a total of four in the Byrne family. Weighing in at six pounds and eight ounces at Valley View Hospital, Ann Jill is ready to play the game of life. It may not be baseball or basketball, but it will be a bawl game from now on, and what a game it will be. Maybe she won't be a table tennis wizard like her mother, and she may think that she is just a basketball after she is tossed around a little. Mrs. Byrne, known as Frances to her many friends in Ada, was society editor for the News, but resigned her position in 1944 to go with her husband to Mt. Pleasant, Texas, where he was employed. She has been making her home in Ada for the past several months. The proud mother was the writer of 'Side Byrnes,' a column that appeared on the society page of the News. Just one day before the birthday of Beverly, who is almost*

a grown-up in the family now, the new baby was born. We have been waiting and wondering for several days, and now the news can be spread around.

As Mother prepared for us to leave the hospital, she gave Beverly, my fifteen-year-old sister, written instructions of what she would need: one Vanta shirt, one Vanta gown, and one Vanta blanket. Vanta was a name brand for a utilitarian cotton line of baby clothes particularly suitable for an infant going home on a snowy day. When Beverly arrived at the hospital with a cute, lacy shirt and a frilly gown, Mother was as angry as could be and uncharacteristically frustrated with Beverly. It seems Beverly had misinterpreted the note to be, "I want a shirt, I want a gown, and I want a blanket." In spite of the gaffe, Mother and I made it home.

My mother, Frances Helen Woolley, was born September 29, 1908, on her parents' farm near Stanton, Alabama, the ninth of eleven children (six girls and five boys). Early on, Frances knew she wanted little to do with her family, farming, or Alabama. She saw education as her path to freedom, and her drive to better herself academically became her lifelong passion.

Frances' family lacked the funds to send her to finishing school, but she was somehow able to attend Auburn, where she acquired enough credits to qualify for a teacher's certificate. Frances' older sister had been offered a teaching position in Okemah, Oklahoma, but subsequently received a better offer from a school in Wyoming. Frances came to Okemah in 1925 with the intention of being offered her sister's position. The school system was desperate for teachers, so they hired her. Within a year, Frances did so well that she was named the school's principal.

Frances was a Southern beauty with jet-black hair, olive skin, green eyes, and an hourglass figure. She was a knockout. Athletically wired, five-foot-four, and weighing a trim one hundred pounds, she turned the boys' heads. She had a light, trilling laugh. Though Southern bred and raised, unlike her family, she had not a trace of a Southern accent. Rather, her diction was pure and clean. Her siblings would call it "better than." She was a flirt, actually coquettish, but she would never do anything inappropriate. She loved to project an allure, like Mary Pickford, a movie star of her day. In addition to her good looks, Frances was an excellent ballroom dancer and piano player. My sister, Beverly, fifteen years my senior, inherited all of Frances' talents and charms. I inherited few.

In Okemah, Frances had enough education to qualify for her provisional teaching certification. During the summer recess of 1926, she enrolled in summer school at East Central Teachers' College in Ada, Oklahoma, in pursuit of her bachelor's degree. Soon after coming to town, she caught the eye of Clifford C. Byrne. Clifford, at five-foot-nine and one hundred thirty pounds, had a dark complexion, a full head of black hair combed straight back, and dark brown, kind eyes. The same way she did for the guys, he turned the ladies' heads. Clifford smoked Camels. Frances preferred Lucky Strikes.

Clifford noticed the new teacher attending summer school at East Central, and it didn't take him long to ask Frances for a date. He knew she rented a room on East Main Street, and he arranged to pick her up there one evening at six o'clock. She dressed in her finest for the occasion. When he knocked on her door, she opened it to see Clifford in a white, double-breasted suit and a straw hat. He smelled of Old Spice. Frances thought he was the most gorgeous thing she had ever seen. Clifford had borrowed the family Model A. He escorted Frances to the front seat, crank-started the car, and got in to drive. They took off down Main Street, a dirt road at that time. Frances' heart raced as she sat next to him. As they drove by Hensler's Drug Store, Frances wondered why they weren't stopping for a Coke. They drove a bit further past the McSwain Movie Theater, and Frances wondered why they weren't stopping for a movie. Clifford hadn't even slowed down. Instead, he motored to the end of West Main Street to the outskirts of Ada, where he pulled over to park and stopped the engine.

Frances looked at Clifford with disdain and said, "What's going on here? Don't you lay a hand on me, Clifford Byrne. That's not the way it's going to be!"

Clifford, a man of few words, replied, "Okay."

He got out, cranked the car, got in, turned it around, and then drove back down Main Street. They went past McSwain's and Hensler's. He matter-of-factly took her home. That was the end of the first date. A few days later, he took her out on a real one.

After a courtship of respectable time, Clifford and Frances were married on January 10, 1930, in Shawnee, some forty-five miles from Ada. A snowstorm curtailed their plans for a weekend honeymoon in Oklahoma City. After marrying, Frances quit her teaching job in Oke-mah, and Clifford was hired as a teller at Ada's First National Bank. They lived in a garage apartment a few blocks from what would be my childhood home.

P.A. Norris owned the bank where Clifford worked. P.A. and his wife, Josephine, were one of Ada's first families. Originally a cotton farmer, P.A. acquired a great deal of land, established the bank, and built a palatial home overlooking a beautiful valley. They had a daugh-ter, Marjorie, and five sons, all of whom would die tragic deaths. Then they had another daughter, Susan. P.A.'s son, Frank, was Clifford's best friend, and they both worked at the bank. Two of P.A.'s granddaughters would become my good friends.

On January 13, 1931, Beverly was born. She had Clifford's color-ing, brown eyes, and blonde hair. She was a beautiful baby and easy to care for. As she progressed in school, she excelled in everything, includ-ing academics, music, and athletics. She lived up to every expectation placed on her. She developed into a striking girl who stood five-foot-six and weighed a slim one hundred pounds. She had olive skin. Well-proportioned, she had long, shapely legs. The PE teacher swore her posture was perfect. She was popular with everyone. While always in the middle of whatever was going on, she never caused her parents a minute's worth of worry.

Beverly's writing talents took off early when she was featured in the *Ada Evening News* as the sixth-grade editor of the *Wee Willard News*. Years later, even her letters home were anticipated and enjoyed as she hilariously captured the mundane aspects of daily life.

My parents were notified by telegram when Beverly was crowned Lake Queen, the ultimate award of Camp Lake Hubert in Minnesota. Back home, she was elected the Sweetheart of DeMolay.

Though Beverly did not stay long enough to graduate from Okla-homa University before marrying a Missouri boy she met at camp, she pledged Kappa Alpha Theta and made an impact as a finalist for Miss OU Freshman.

Mary Little Gurley, one of Beverly's contemporaries, talked about seeing a side of Beverly I never knew existed. One day, when Mary and her friend Margaret walked up the wide staircase at the Theta house, Beverly came down carrying a bag of popcorn in her left hand. Margaret loved to challenge the status quo. Beverly personified the status quo, seemingly too good to be true. Margaret reached out and hit the bottom of Beverly's popcorn sack, sending a blizzard of kernels skyward. Before the popcorn hit the stairs, Beverly smacked her right hand against Margaret's cheek so hard that the Thetas on both floors heard the slap. Margaret never crossed Beverly again.

Mary also said that Frances was determined for Beverly to stand out as soon as possible at OU. Beverly's letters home tended to downplay scholastics and highlight her social impact on campus:

In a little chat with my English teacher the other day, she informed me that my themes thus far had been very good but that I always selected such strange, intangible topics that she often wondered if I possessed any knowledge about writing on the common things of life. It seems she always writes 'Very good!' at the end of my paper and then plops a C or B- at the top for some disastrous comma fault or the atrocity of misspelling a word.

Congratulations are well in order in one phase at least. Guess what? I did write a new song for the variety show. Surprise! During the last few days, I whipped up a new one involving and dwelling upon the difficulties of getting a date from the masculine viewpoint with the ratio of seven-to-one here at OU. Whether it is too good or not, I don't know, but at least it's appropriate! Am sending you a copy of this morning's Daily. Note the feeble smile I managed to muster after the photographer aimed the camera at me and counted to sixty.

During Beverly's sophomore year, she collaborated with Frances on a musical act for the Sooners Scandals, the all-school talent show. Beverly sang and played a revised-for-college-life version of "Hard-hearted Hannah." Frances did not know that Beverly chose to wear white shorts and high heels accentuating her shapely figure. When she finished playing and stood up from the piano, the audience went wild. There was not a soul on campus that did not know who Beverly Byrne was. She was frequently invited to repeat her performance at special campus events. By 1950, she had cut a record playing and singing "My Heart Belongs to Daddy."

The only time I heard of an instance when Beverly got in trouble was during her first year at OU when she and four of her sorority sisters went to Austin, Texas, for the weekend. They stayed on campus at the Theta house. On Saturday, they took off on a shopping spree downtown. The other girls came from families where money was not an issue. Mother had given Beverly a blank check so she could get a little something. Caught up in the group frenzy, Beverly used her check to purchase a three-piece wool suit. When Daddy heard just how much his daughter had spent, tears welled in his eyes. That one outfit cost more than half of what he had earned in the previous month. Mother insisted he have a talk with Beverly and come to an understanding regarding her careless spending.

Daddy called Beverly aside when she came home the following weekend.

"Beverly, your mother thought it would be a good idea for the two of us to come to an understanding. Do you understand?" he asked.

"Yes, Daddy. I understand," she replied.

Daddy dealt out correction with an economy of words.

Beverly was a tough sibling to follow. If there had not been so many years between us, I'm not sure I would have been able to like her. It was no help when high school teachers recalled mundane specifics about Beverly in class long ago, including the lovely ivory cameo she wore on a black velvet ribbon or where she sat in the classroom. Teachers didn't talk about any of my friends' siblings to that detail. Still, I adored her, and I felt special to be her little sister.

Frances became society editor for the *Ada Evening News*. Clifford's sister had been in this position. When she left Ada, Frances was allowed to assume her role. As the society editor, she constantly found ways to feature Beverly's accomplishments.

Frances had beautiful, flowing handwriting. Though left-handed, she held her pen like right-handers, rather than over the top as many left-handers were taught to do. She was Ada's Lois Lane, looking and listening for the latest in Ada's society news and visiting intently with those she met. Frances was all business. She was very prim. Like her firstborn, she had perfect posture. She wore high heels and hose. She usually wore shirtwaist dresses that accentuated her well-proportioned figure. She preferred navy, red, black, and white. Her clothes were mostly solids and stripes with very few florals. Frances parted her shoulder-length pageboy on the left, and she sported a tortoiseshell barrette. She and her best friend, Thena McBride, enjoyed keeping up with the young crowd, and their homes were often gathering places for a Coke, piano music, and conversation.

Life was grand for the Byrnes. Clifford was doing well in his job at the bank, Frances loved her role as mother and society editor, and Beverly was a perfect daughter. But everything changed in a heart-beat, that is, the heartbeat of a baby girl in Frances' womb. As Beverly began her sophomore year at Ada High, Frances, at the age of thirty-seven, learned she was pregnant. Having to share this news with family, friends, and especially Beverly made Frances' sexual activity humiliat-ingly public. Frances and Beverly were just sick about the news. I never learned of Clifford's reaction to it.

Upon hearing the news of Frances' pregnancy, her associates at the newspaper decorated her office with balloons and pink crepe paper in celebration. When she walked in, she began dismantling what had been done. In her mind, celebration was not appropriate.

Frances was traumatized by the pregnancy that sucked the wind out of her midlife sails. Clifford was a rising star at the bank and eager to climb socially. Frances, however, was so ashamed that she would never again attempt to move forward on Ada's social ladder. She was livid that her life had taken a detour from where she had hoped it would go, and Clifford and I were to blame.

"Honey, Come Here"

1992

"HONEY, COME HERE. COME HERE. Come here. Come here."

"Is somebody talking to me?" I thought. "Must be. Without my glasses, I can't be sure."

A shriveled lady with curly, gray hair and I were alone in the hall of the Summerhill Psychiatric Hospital in Tulsa, Oklahoma. She would have fit right in with the residents in the nursing home where my mother was waiting out her final days. It was November 1992, my third time in a psych ward. Not only was I pacing the hall because I was desperate for sleep, I was also getting away from my roommate, Fran, who talked incessantly about slop jars. I tried, but I could not have gotten a word in edgewise about my ability to see inside my brain. Because I was the only forty-something in here, the staff placed me in geriatrics as opposed to the drug and alcohol wing. I was getting the drift that all here, patients and staff, had their own agendas and could care less about mine.

"Yeah, I guess she's talking to me," I thought. "What should I do? I've only been a patient here since pre-dawn hours, not long enough to know the rules."

As I started toward her wheelchair I wondered if she was in restraints. If so, could I be next?

"What's the matter with you?" she asked.

"Not a thing, but thanks for asking," I replied. "Actually I have had the distinct honor to see the inside of my brain and it is so spectacular that any day I expect to be contacted by the scientific community for an interview to..."

"Big deal," she said. "I just returned from a voyage on the Seven Seas. Come closer. I want to tell you a secret."

I leaned down ready to receive her adulation that never came.

"If you don't shut up," she whispered, "I, Sheba the Great, will send the mighty Sinbad to silence you. Remember, dear, you are not safe anywhere in this place."

I backed away with question marks doing split kicks in my mind. I saw myself running down the hall. As I crossed the finish line, freeing myself of mental illness, my head would go back, and my toes would touch my hair in celebration. It was such a wonderful feeling to be flowing along as fast and well as I was. I just wished I could find someone on the outside who was ready to confirm this as real and not mania.

The next afternoon, spent of energy, I lay tearful in bed. The treatment around here seemed arbitrary. I felt as if I was being punished.

"Punished for what?" I thought. "Does anyone know how scary it is to be this exhausted and still unable to sleep?"

To ease my chest pain, somebody on the staff delivered the ice I requested. Recycling my small milk carton from lunch, I devised a custom ice pack. I ran the ice-filled carton slowly up and down my chest, from my neck to my waist. The freezing cold carton reminded me that all I'd like right now was a Coke with a lot of ice.

"Could someone check me out of here, if for only an hour?" I thought. "We could go for a little ride out to get one? Hello? Is anyone listening? Does anyone care?"

Mississippi Avenue

1946–1951

CLIFFORD AND FRANCES BROUGHT ME home to 217 North Mississippi, a tiny two-bedroom, white, wooden house with a boxwood hedge around the front. I'm told that I cried a lot as a baby. There are pictures of me in my buggy, and most show me doing so. I know that, even though Beverly continued to bring joy into the Byrne household, Mother's anger raged with her lot in life, and she was slow to forgive Daddy. Though she rarely raised her voice, her eyes could spit fire.

When I was two, Frank Norris died in a plane crash. Daddy, reeling from the sadness of losing his best friend and realizing his main proponent at the bank was gone, decided to go into business for himself as an independent oil and gas lease broker under the tutelage of Rudy Roodhouse. This move resulted in a significant lifestyle change for our family. As Beverly finished high school and set off for sorority rush at Oklahoma University, Daddy left for his first of many leasing assignments that would take him on the road for months at a time. Losing daily contact with the two most nurturing people in my life at the same time may account for the look of bewilderment that shows in my eyes in the few photos available from that era. Left home alone with a two-year-old, Mother was distraught at best and mad as hell at worst. Though her anger was primarily toward Daddy, there was no one there to feel it but me. His occupational shift to long periods of travel may have been the best solution he could find to save their marriage. She was hot with fury, so he found a way to stay out of the kitchen.

Daddy trading his predictable career path at the bank for the more exotic life of professional travel irritated Mother. She especially disliked evenings without Cliff because he wasn't home to take me on long car rides that gave her a bit of relief. Mother dreaded storms, which were plentiful in Ada throughout the summer. One late night, when ear-splitting thunder claps of an approaching storm awakened Mother, she plucked me from my bed and carried me as fast as she could go for the two blocks to the Armstrong's house. Streak lightning lit the whole way. My blanket was soaked by the time we reached the safety of their porch.

About the age of two, I refused to drink milk. This particular resistance remained intact for about ten years. An incident of projectile vomiting of Milk of Magnesia may have been largely responsible for my intense resolve. As a finicky eater, I associated all red foods with my dislike for tomatoes and never touched a bite of watermelon until junior high. Naptime and bedtime were always a challenge for my mother and me. I never went to sleep gladly. Mother was as determined as I was, so I was often on the receiving end of switchings for my resistive behavior.

Saying Mother was driven would be a gross understatement. When I was three, she must have written a letter to her older sister, Margaret, in which she shared the troubles in her life. Margaret's reply indicated how worried she was for Mother:

You certainly have your hands full. I wish you would give up some of your activity, as I'm afraid that you are overdoing it. I'll be really glad when you write me that you have entered some kind of health program for yourself with proper food and relaxation as the chief consideration. As one enters the forties, it is well to take things easy if possible. I would be so happy to know that you had stopped pushing yourself from one activity to another.

She ended her letter:

Do write again when you have a little time on your hands. I wish so much that you would begin to take a little better care of yourself than your letter indicates you are doing.

I was of average size for my age. I wore my brown hair with bangs and braids. Against my wishes, Mother washed my hair in the kitchen sink using Luster Crème shampoo that came in a blue jar. My back and head ached from lying against the hard, linoleum countertop and cold, porcelain sink. With the first splash of water on my face, I squirmed and howled until the threat of giving me "something to howl about" convinced me to reduce my wails to a whimper. To get a high shine, the final rinse was with vinegar. There was no such thing as conditioner to tame the tangles. I felt Mother's long, thin fingers running through my hair to make a grating squeak. This weekly activity was an ordeal for both of us.

There were no children of my age in our neighborhood, and I don't recall having a playmate or friend until kindergarten when I met Barbara Harris and Lynn Ramsay. I lived a solitary life. Beverly sometimes took me places with her. At the downtown drug store, I enjoyed climbing up on those seats at the counter to twirl around and around with a Coke while she visited with her friends. But social interaction like that happened infrequently.

Because we were a one-car family, as most were in those days, Mother and I walked everywhere when Daddy was out of town. Our house was centrally located. We were within reasonable walking distance to most places, but I, nonetheless, whined while walking behind her. Frances, an excellent pianist, played for Thena McBride's dance studio. In exchange, Thena didn't charge Frances for my dance lessons. One of our frequent hikes was to Thena's, where I sat through innumerable practices and performances. I often camped out under the piano with Thena's son, Bert. Annual recitals were held at the McSwain Theater, where, as the youngest pupil, I was saved for the last act with Bert. They said I threw up before we went onstage to dance to "Ballin' the Jack." Even though performing came naturally to Beverly, it never came naturally to me. In fact, Thena considered me one of the two worst dancers in her studio's history.

My stage fright manifested itself in public, too. One day, as Mother and I stood under the bank clock on the corner of Main and Broadway, she turned to introduce me to friends she had met.

Mother said, "This is my daughter, Jill."

Right then, I picked up her skirt and slipped under it. With the swiftness of a magician pulling a rabbit out of a hat, Mother jerked her dress down and me out from under it without missing a beat in her conversation. Back home, Mother put her purse down on the dining room chair next to the piano and then headed out the back door. She was going to the hedge next to the alley. When I heard the screen door slam, I knew trouble was ahead. Peeking out the dining room window, I saw her ripping leaves off her switch as she walked back toward the house. I was already in a dance of anxiety by the time Mother grabbed my arm, twisting my squirming form around for her switch to find the back of my legs.

"Don't you ever pull my dress up in public again! Do you hear?" she yelled.

While she spoke, she swatted me for good measure. The volume of my sobs and inability to respond let her know that her lesson got through to me.

We lived a short distance from King's Market. My mother and I were frequent shoppers there, and Mr. and Mrs. King often leaned over the counter to give me a treat. I longed for the day I could see the top of that counter. The butcher, Happy, always had a kind word for me. I felt pretty much at home at King's. Many times, Mother sent me there to buy a loaf of bread so we could have pineapple sandwiches for lunch. She called ahead to say I was coming and to make arrangements to pay later. My simple responsibility was to take the bread they gave me and carry it home. I was tremendously proud to be so trusted. No matter how carefully the Kings cautioned me not to squeeze the bread, I always arrived home clutching the loaf to my body so tightly that it lost its shape. When mother saw the misshapen loaf of bread, her brow furrowed, her lips pursed, and she glared at me as if I had committed an unpardonable sin.

"Can't you even carry bread?" she hissed.

I hung my head in shame. She was right. I failed to deliver the simplest things she asked of me. I could not even carry bread.

Through some measure of serendipity, I had the good fortune to have five baby chicks come into my life. They stayed sheltered in a cardboard box under my back steps. Not only were these chicks the softest, most squeezable things I had ever encountered, each was dyed a different color of red, green, blue, purple, and pink. Yes, I was cautioned to leave them alone and just look, but the temptation to hold one was more than I could withstand. By Easter Sunday, they were all dead. Though the dye may have contributed to their early demise, I believed I had killed them by holding them and loving them too much, much as I had squeezed the loaves of bread into misshapen lumps.

I knew my home on 217 North Mississippi was important because Officer Blue was assigned nearby to stop traffic for kids going to school. Because I often waited on the corner for him, he made me his official helper, a job I took very seriously because I had yet to begin school. We worked side by side for quite a while.

One day, while he waited for kids to cross, a man rolled down his car window and loudly asked, "Officer Blue, who's your little helper?"

I already knew what Officer Blue was going to say, "Oh, that's Jill Byrne, Frances and Clifford Byrne's little girl. She's my helper, and I don't know what I'd do without her."

Jarred back to reality, I heard Officer Blue saying, "Oh, this is Jill the Pill!"

My anger and embarrassment swept me past Officer Blue, amid his protests, where I bunkered in behind a nearby hedge, lobbing an occasional rock toward the corner.

"How dare Officer Blue make fun of me!" I thought.

I decided not to help him again.

The legend of high school football in Ada established itself after World War II when it began a reputation of grooming future stars for the Oklahoma Sooners. Those Friday night games were community events that Mother continued to attend even in Daddy's absence. Norris Stadium was nestled in a valley just east of and below the main campus of East Central Teachers' College. On the hill between the campus and the stadium, there was an elaborate rock garden containing a small stream that had been a WPA project. The promise of spending time there was the carrot my mother offered as we walked to the games.

The last time the two of us attended together was memorable. During the game, I fell asleep in her lap. Mother became caught up in the excitement of the close game. When the mighty Cougars scored, she jumped up with the crowd, oblivious to the still figure she saw flying off her lap. In the confusion, she dove to break my fall, taking the full physical hit as we landed a couple rows down from where we started. I recall fans standing and yelling. No one helped us to our feet. We left immediately with my mother limping and crying quietly. She never attended another high school football game.

To keep her company while Daddy was away, Mother rented out my bedroom to female students attending East Central. One spring, Daddy came home briefly from North Dakota. I was so glad to see him. He gave me a piece of stick candy as he got out of the car. As we were going up the back steps, the college girl staying with us was on her way to hang clothes on our clothesline. When I stepped on her robe, I flew face-first into the cement step, instantly breaking my two front teeth. The stick candy lodged in my gum where my teeth had been. It was typical of Daddy's and my luck. He had been home only a minute. Mother was hopping mad. She was so upset that she left him and me alone to deal with the problem. Daddy phoned our family dentist, Dr. Goff, who agreed to meet us at his office immediately. As he sped downtown, I stood on the car seat next to Daddy. (Seat belts were nonexistent those days.) I looked in the rearview mirror and saw the candy dangling from my mouth. Though it hurt, I wasn't crying. I had stopped crying when Mother became angry with Daddy.

In my early youth, the Byrnes were Presbyterians. They became Episcopalians about the time I entered grade school. The Presbyterian Church had a grand entrance with about twenty wide, smooth, concrete steps. Daddy, Mother, and I attended church on most Sundays. One Sunday, he let Mother sleep in, and just the two of us went. He had little experience in all the negotiations necessary for getting a four-year-old presentably dressed and ready to go. As long as I put on clothes, he really didn't care what I wore, so I took maximum advantage of the moment. I put on one red sock and one yellow sock. I also put on two shiny, black tap shoes. My soul can still catch the rhythm of tapping up all those steps and down a slick, marble aisle toward our pew. Mother was mortified to see what I had worn when we returned home.

When I was five, Beverly married Bob Taylor of Columbia, Missouri. Mother was stressed from the day they announced their engagement. Unrelated to the occasion, months before the wedding, Mother made arrangements with the lumber company to send a carpenter out to build some shelves. No specific date was set. With the wedding date approaching, she forgot about it. A day or so before the ceremony, she realized that neither she nor Daddy would have time to mow our yard, so she called the employment agency to find someone to do the job.

Late that afternoon, someone knocked at the door.

A man said, "Mrs. Byrne."

She cut through his introduction, saying, "I'm too busy to talk. Will you go ahead and start mowing in the back?"

"But Mrs. Byrne—" he said.

Again, she interrupted, "There's no time to talk about it."

Later, he tried to speak to her. Again, she would not listen. Finally, he came to the door with his job well-done.

Mother asked, "What do I owe you?" (Remember that we're talking about 1951 here.)

The man replied, "Thirty-five dollars!"

Mother screamed in disbelief.

The man said, "Lady, I don't mow yards. I tried to tell you that I'm a carpenter."

Cliff's friends were quick on the phone to her, soliciting an opportunity to get her mowing account. Mother was not amused then or ever by this incident.

Beverly's wedding came off with only one hitch. I, the five-year-old flower girl, balked of course. I loved the pink, dotted Swiss dress and being included, but, when it was time for me to start down the aisle, everyone turned to the back. With all eyes on me, I refused to move, paralyzed with stage fright. Had someone thought to bribe me as I see couples do now, I might have made it. Pictures of the wedding party include me with my feet wide apart, arms folded, and my face unsmiling. Beverly's disappointment with my behavior that evening grew through the years. The black-and-white wedding photos bring out the intensity in my mother's eyes, but they miss the equal intensity of her deep purple dress.

For Frances, with Beverly leaving home, Clifford taking to the road, and me there to care for, it must have seemed to her that time stood still. She seemed happiest when playing the piano in our dining room or the pump organ in our living room. In my line of vision, I saw two small, square, Oriental motif ashtrays at each end of the piano. I enjoyed playing with them, but I was always cautioned to leave them alone.

While she played, I was required to sit at my little wooden desk near her. She encouraged me to work on my numbers and letters. My penmanship was rarely up to her standards, and my form was constantly in question.

In second grade, I remember hearing her say, "Of course she can't write. She doesn't even know how to hold a pencil."

This was reinforced when a teacher assigned me to write sentences with my spelling words.

Frances was quick to recognize their mundane nature and said, "Here, let me see if I can jazz them up a bit."

She could and did all the way through my high school years.

To pass the time and keep up with current events, Mother read voraciously. Our radio was in the kitchen. When Mother made lunch, she insisted I keep quiet so she could listen to Paul Harvey. On Saturday mornings, when Mother cleaned house, my main job was to stay out of her way.

Most children would get to swim in the summertime to escape Ada's sweltering heat and humidity. Mother, however, had a deathly fear of water. At a creek on their farm, one of her siblings held Mother's head underwater for too long, and she nearly drowned. I never saw her swim. Though she would have been striking in one, I don't believe she owned a bathing suit. Though she repeatedly enrolled me in swim lessons at the college, my progress was marginal. Terror of water was just one of many fears she instilled in me.

Because we lived on a busy street, I usually played in the backyard or on the north side of the house. As I came down the back steps, there was a redbud tree that provided a shady place to play. The ground was hardpacked there, cool and damp with patches of moss. While digging was my favorite pastime, I was careful not to dig too deep lest I might dig to the other side, fall through it, and go off the earth.

I told myself, "No, I will not allow myself to dig as deeply as I really wish to go."

The Bumpers

1951–1958

UEL BUMPERS WAS THE KEYSTONE of my time at 1110 East Eighth Street. After years of therapy as an adult, I added the moniker of "my second mother" to his name. In many ways, Uel was a male version of Frances. Both were intelligent and well-read. They were polar opposites politically, and each seemed to enjoy the stimulation of frequent verbal jousts on issues of the day. Yet, in general, Uel was as low-key as Frances was high-strung.

Ellen and Uel Bumpers were married in the summer of 1942. She was a Texas native who was divorced with a sixteen-year-old daughter, Betty. Up to this time, Uel had been a confirmed bachelor. My theory would be that Ellen's cooking weakened his resolve and filled out his lanky frame. That lady could cook!

Frances and Ellen became friends prior to my birth. Ellen operated her own beauty parlor, which became a ready source of the latest information for Frances' society page.

Years later, Ellen remembered visiting with Frances on Mississippi Avenue when I approached her and said, "It's dark and time for you to go home."

She had come to tell Frances that her next-door neighbors on Eighth Street were moving. She thought the Byrnes might want to look at the house and consider a neighborhood with children for me. So we moved.

Ellen and Uel were both thirty-six when they married. Remarkably, eight years later, their one and only child, Jane Elizabeth, was born. No two parents could have doted more than they did on Janie. Uel had inherited and managed property in town and several farms nearby. Consequently, throughout his adult life, he was active in the

Pontotoc County Soil Conservation Bureau. In the late 1950s, Cliff convinced him to join in some occasional leasing out of state. Uel really didn't work much, allowing him to be very much a hands-on-dad with Janie.

It was to my great advantage to have next-door neighbors a couple of years older than Frances who were ecstatic to have a daughter four years younger than me. I strongly believe their parental enthusiasm tempered my mother's vocal despair for being an older mother. Ellen laid out three square meals a day and effortlessly accomplished daily domestic chores while actively serving on the League of Women Voters, participating in her church circle, and playing bridge regularly.

Uel was relatively handy, but, more than anything, he was there with Janie. Most likely, I was there as well. I was with them so often there were people in town who thought I was a member of the Bumpers family. Whatever projects he undertook, he included us both. He planted two young elm trees and rigged an elaborate watering system. I stood with him many a day as he watered through the grueling Oklahoma summer heat. In their backyard, he devised a tire swing and provided push power while teaching us to pump.

Every spring, Uel freshened up Janie's sandbox. He arranged for a well-placed floodlight to illuminate both backyards.

In 1955, I gave Uel and Janie the chicken pox for Christmas. That little gift turned into a major event for a man of fifty years. We documented his illness with their movie camera, and he bared his chest for a close-up of his misery. I was the only guest allowed at their house for their family festivities, which was the year Janie received a record player from Santa.

Two years earlier, I had readily dispelled the Santa myth with Janie one winter night as we went from my house to hers. This was news she did not gladly receive. Instead, she went running and crying to her mother, earning me a hasty departure and immediate spanking from my mother.

Mother said, "Just because you think you are so smart. You have no business telling Janie there is no Santa. I can assure you that he will never darken your door again."

Mother made good on her word. From then on, I never saw another gift or remembrance from him. The pain of this was compounded annually with the generosity of the jolly old man at the Bumpers' house. Over the years, Janie received an abundance of gifts from Santa, including the first 78-RPM record player on our block; a shiny, new bicycle; a red-topped play table with two folding chairs, and eight plastic melody bells.

More than once, Frances entered the city's Christmas light decoration contest. She won it all on at least one occasion. One year, the candles in the front yard were all taller than I was. Her talents spilled over to the Bumpers' porch when she blackened their front windows to set off a nativity scene she cut out freehand. I always wanted to be of some help on these projects, but I was generally just in the way.

Ellen and Uel felt Frances did not feed me enough. When I arrived at their kitchen door during supper, they invited me to join them.

I said, "Yes, I'd like just a little bit."

They had scrumptious homemade desserts. At our house, an occasional bowl of red Jell-O was excitement, but nothing compared to those meringue pies, three-layer cakes with white icing, fruit cobblers, and homemade ice cream next door.

In the summer of 1952, I was six, and Janie had recently turned two. While she wasn't much fun to play with yet, I enjoyed helping the Bumpers take care of her. Often after Janie woke from her nap, Ellen would let me select from a myriad of choices a fresh pastel dress for her to wear. One especially hot summer afternoon, I was intent on taking Janie over to my house. Ellen was less than enthusiastic because she was too busy to stop and put on Janie's shoes.

She pointed out, "The pavement would be much too hot for Janie's feet."

I said, "I'll carry Janie across the driveway."

She asked, "How will you open your front door?"

I quickly responded, "I'll put Janie down on the doormat while I open the door.'

Once she reluctantly agreed, Janie and I were off. Meeting the first challenge, I was able to lug Janie safely across the single-lane driveway. I gathered her up again near the sun-exposed porch. Just after I navigated us up the two front steps, I realized the doormat was not in its accustomed place. I looked around and spotted it on the sidewalk near the first step. I promised Ellen I would put Janie on the mat while I opened the door, so I put Janie down on that sizzling cement while I raced down to get the mat. Her bloodcurdling screams as the bottoms of her baby feet burned simply froze me in my tracks as Ellen swept by and Frances rushed out.

After the Bumpers' car pulled out of the driveway, Mother grabbed me by the arm and marched me inside the house. She went straight to the refrigerator and reached on top where she kept a switch on reserve. (While I may have mentioned my mother was left-handed, I failed to add that she batted right-handed and also dealt her punishment the same.) The switch was not fresh, so, when I reached back in a futile attempt to protect my legs, the switch snapped in my grasp. Mother's fury escalated while she spanked me repeatedly with her hand. My tears continued long after she marched me down the hall.

"You get in this bedroom. Don't you come out until I say!" she said.

I didn't leave the house for days. The spanking and grounding I received did not touch the anguish I felt when I peeked out the front bedroom window to watch the Bumpers wheel Janie up and down the block with her feet bandaged in two big, white balls of gauze. Ellen and Uel both tried to comfort me. They knew it was an accident for which I was sorry. But Frances stayed mad and said I was stupid. My suffering was interminable for the time it took Janie to heal and finally walk again. Frances never acknowledged the event as an accident or the honest mistake of a well-intentioned six-year-old.

Little Sympathy

I N THE FALL OF 1952, I was enrolled in the first grade at Willard School. My teacher was Miss Mae Bentley, who was equal in height to the average sixth-grader. Though gentle and soft-spoken, her students knew she meant business. My friends, Barbara and Lynn, were also in my class. That year, my mother gave her light green upright piano to the school, and it was placed in Miss Bentley's room. My mother would occasionally come to our class and play while leading us in singing games. My all-time favorite song was "Rig-a-Jig-Jig." At the peak of this game, a partner and I skipped around the circle of classmates as fast as we could. My braids with satin ribbons flew behind me when I was chosen to skip. My mother seemed happiest when she was playing a lively song. She often threw back her head and laughed as she hit the final chord. Seeing her so happy, I begged her to play it again.

Elementary school cafeterias did not exist in Ada, so we either brought our lunch or went home to eat. One day, I decided to go home for lunch and invited a friend to come with me. When we arrived at my door, Mother was not home. I don't remember what we did for food, but, within a block of our return to school, Mother's car slowly approached. She said nothing, but her glare let me know she was unhappy. Soon after class resumed, an office worker came to our door and said I was being called to the office. This was not a common event in first grade. I didn't know enough to be scared. I instead felt somewhat important to have been singled out.

Much to my surprise, the principal, Mrs. Antoinette Huff, a portly woman with her hair in a sizable bun, looked sternly at me and said, "Your mother called me to report that she has seen you off the school grounds."

Mrs. Huff's size alone was intimidating, and her message of following school rules was duly received. I returned to class visibly chagrined. I felt added shame that my mother had reported me. I never left the grounds without permission again.

Early in life, I learned I wouldn't get much sympathy from Mother when I was under the weather. Whenever I showed the slightest sign of feeling low, for example, hanging my head or resting it drowsily on my hand, Mother laughed a nervous trill. It wasn't a compassionate laugh. Instead, I sensed that my impending sickness somehow reflected poorly on her, so I vowed never to show her how bad I felt. Many a time I hid out of her sight, curled up with a stomachache.

One early spring day, I walked home from Willard School for lunch. My plate was on the table. After one sniff, I recognized my mother's egg salad sandwiches, which ran a close second to my favorite pineapple ones. I ate silently while she stood at the sink, staring blankly out the window. This was her usual stance while she listened to Paul Harvey give the news. Years before, I had been trained not to interrupt until he said, "Good day!" By now, I had choked down my lunch. I was heading out the front door, eager to get back to school in time to join my friends on the playground.

The three blocks back to Willard were on relatively level terrain yet slightly downhill. The last two blocks were tree-shaded and treacherous to navigate because the roots of the huge, old trees buckled the sidewalks. However, this first-grader displayed nimble prowess as I skipped back down Ninth Street with my pigtails flying behind me.

Something came over me just before Miss Bentley dismissed us for the day. I didn't feel so good. Every so often, I tasted the egg salad lunch again. My stomach hurt, so I didn't skip home. I trudged back up Ninth Street and then crossed over to Eighth on Highland.

"I'm home," I said weakly as I opened the front door. "I'll be outside."

"That's good," my mother replied from the hall as she paused from her conversation with Thena on the phone.

Out of her sight worked best. Choosing a clump of clover west of the garage as a resting place, I kicked off my shoes. Not even the lure of white flowers perfect for a daisy chain could distract me from my physical discomfort and regular burps of egg salad.

In time, Mother called me inside. She was busy in the kitchen. I grabbed a throw pillow and slithered behind the sofa, giving literal meaning to lying low. The coolness of the sateen-covered pillow on my flushed cheek gave momentary relief as I waited and hoped my pain would diminish before I was discovered.

Eventually, night fell. Mother told me to come eat supper. Worriedly, I stirred the contents on my plate while I propped my head with my left hand. I sensed eating one bite would cause the egg salad to come out. It was too risky.

"Well, if you are not going to finish your supper, you can just go on to bed," my mother said as she began to clear the table.

As long as I stubbornly refused to admit weakness, she, too, was willing to deny.

"Okay," I said thankfully.

I was in bed with the lights out in record time and without discussion, but I still had that recurrent taste of egg salad. The long night gave me time to practice being really still as my stomach roiled on.

I stirred my way through breakfast. With determination, I made the walk to Willard just in time to step into Miss Bentley's room and throw up yesterday's lunch. Miss Bentley did not laugh, but I felt a whole lot better.

Sometime during first grade, I came down with an infection, and the doctor gave me penicillin. As a result of the penicillin shot, I broke out in an angry red, scaly rash that ran from the bottom of my feet to the top of my head. Though I never took penicillin again, this same outbreak randomly reoccurred. It was usually misdiagnosed as measles for at least the first week. By second grade, I was taken to Oklahoma City to see a skin specialist for treatment, which included lying naked in a dark room with ultra-ray light.

As if these treatments were not humiliating enough, frequent sunbaths in the nude were prescribed and carried out in my backyard. Placing blankets on the clothesline, Frances set up a screen. She left me out there, bare and alone, until my raw screams penetrated the walls of the house when a plane flew overhead. Having my classmates call me "Measles" added to my self-consciousness.

My mother regularly covered each sore with an odorous, brown liquid and added an oatmeal concoction to my bathwater. Only time seemed to improve these skin eruptions, but Mother reinstated the treatments with each outbreak. At least two of these attacks occurred just before Easter.

Uel Bumpers recorded Easter festivities with his movie camera. I had to stay inside, but I hung out a window in my pajamas while Janie stood nearby in her Easter finery. At the time, there was confusion as to whether I had psoriasis or eczema. I found a letter written in 1954 from the doctor to my mother. It included an article indicating a possible emotional/stress base for psoriasis. Fortunately, I outgrew the massive eruptions.

In second grade, Barbara, Lynn, and I were enrolled in Mrs. Sheggog's room. (Mrs. Sheggog was Miss Bentley's sister. She was just as nice but much taller.) At this point, while Barbara remained nice to both of us, Lynn was aggressive about wanting an exclusionary friendship with Barbara at my expense. Two instances of this theme played out regularly at recess. Lynn would suggest we play hide-and-seek.

"Jill, you go hide. We'll come find you," Lynn would say.

I would lay low in tall grass located near the edge of the playground. I would finally peek out to see my best friends skipping down the sidewalk, hand in hand.

"Jill, we'll go hide. You come find us," Lynn would say.

I would not see them again until the bell rang to return to class.

One day, Barbara and I were holding hands as we lined up after noon recess. Suddenly, I was skidding over the gravel on my stomach as Lynn stepped up to take my place next to Barbara. A teacher witnessed Lynn's tactics and reported it. After recess, the three of us were called out of the room. Lynn was reprimanded. This was one of the few times she was ever corrected for bullying me.

Later that same year, Mrs. Sheggog announced we were going to put on a play for the entire school. She said she was going to assign the parts. Barbara was to be the red egg, and Lynn was to be the blue egg. She went on through the yellow and green eggs.

Then she finally turned to me and said, "Jill, you are pink."

I was immediately crestfallen. All the others were strong, vivid colors. I was plain old pink.

When I could feel no lower, Mrs. Sheggog said, "The play is called the *Little Pink Egg*!"

I've always believed that she gave me the lead role in an effort to counter the effects of Lynn's steamroller approach to friendship.

During second grade, Frances decided to learn to sew. (She came to it naturally with three sisters who were talented with needle and thread. One was a professional seamstress.) She undertook this challenge with the primary focus of developing my wardrobe. She wasn't wearing her glasses when she selected the pattern and material for my first homemade dress, a light lavender outfit with purple trim and buttons. On close inspection, she loudly discovered the hem was scalloped. This was the beginning of tried patience for both of us, though I gained richly through adulthood as she perfected her talent.

Whenever my mother launched into any project, sewing or other, life as I knew it stopped. She hated to be interrupted by any regularly scheduled activity, such as a meal. I was content with some Saltines or Ritz crackers. Sometimes Mother took a break from her project, slapped some grape jelly on a piece of bread to stop my whining, and shoved it my way. I was allowed to eat it on the back steps, where neither of us had to worry about crumbs. After dark, she stopped work on her project long enough to stir up a bowl of oatmeal or cream of wheat for me and heat up last Sunday's leftover cabbage and liver for herself.

When Barbara, Lynn, and I were selected to represent our second-grade class in the school talent show, we performed a tap routine to "School Days" while wearing matching Stewart plaid, full skirts with white eyelet trim and white blouses. Mother made my outfit. The three of us loved to twirl around in these skirts. Mine was a bit different with the addition of sewn suspender straps.

From shirtwaist dresses, squaw dresses, chemises, shifts, pedal pushers, capri pants, Slim Jims, tents, swimsuits, winter coats, and formals, Mother met each fashion challenge with intensity and a drive for perfection. A large piece of me believes that her sewing was her effort to make me stand out as the girl with the cutest clothes because it was obvious I would never stand out as naturally as Beverly.

In fairness to Lynn, her aggressive behavior may have come from her desire to please her mother, who was as demanding as Frances and considerably younger. Like Beverly, Lynn could deliver and I couldn't.

Blue Light Special

Circa 1959

MOTHER, NOT K-MART, FOUNDED THE blue light special.

One late winter afternoon, I turned on a lamp to read and asked, "What's wrong with this light, Mother?"

"Not a thing. Why do you ask?" she replied.

"It's not as bright as it was yesterday," I said.

"That's just your imagination," she said. "I put a blue bulb in that lamp today. I'll have you know that blue bulbs are the newest thing, so get used to them. I bought enough at the grocery store this morning to change out every white one in our house. Now get up and help me replace the one in the ceiling light of your bedroom. And bring the kitchen step stool with you."

I climbed out of my comfortable spot of a chair in the living room with a muted groan of resignation.

Halfway down the hall, my mother said, "I heard that, and I don't appreciate it one bit after all I do for you. For once, you could get with the program."

"I'm coming," I said, getting the step stool out of the pantry closet.

This little ladder had three steps, two that folded into each other and the top one that served as a flat seat. It had been in our house longer than I had been, and it was about thirty inches tall. I wasn't much shorter than Mother, but I was more sure-footed.

"Get up there," she instructed me.

"Okay, Mother, but please don't hold onto my ankles," I said.

"Now, Jill, you know that, if I did not avoid heights, I would jump up there and do it myself," she said. "You can just get used to it. Holding on to you helps me make sure you don't fall and cause me more problems."

"There," I said. "Let go. I'm coming down."

Mother walked over to the door and flipped the overhead switch. She said, "Yes. I think the darker light on these gray walls in your room is fascinating, don't you?"

"Not really," I said. "I think it makes it look a little scary in here."

"That's just your vivid imagination," she said. "You don't have any judgment about good taste."

The next morning, we struck a compromise.

"Mother, as much as I don't like the blue overhead light in my bedroom, I really don't like it here in the kitchen. I think it makes the food look funny," I said.

"Don't get me started about having to raise the world's most finicky eater," she said.

"Okay then," I offered. "I'm willing to live with your blue lights everywhere in the house if you will change back this one in the kitchen."

"That sounds fair," she said.

Once again, what I thought didn't really count.

Young at Heart

RECENTLY FINDING THIS LETTER HAS confirmed the support I always felt from Beverly's corner.

University Of Missouri-Columbia
School of Business and Public Administration
Department of Accounting and Statistics

March 5, 1954

Dearest Mother:

I enjoyed your letter so much yesterday, yet I got so fired up about your trouble with Jill that I decided to sit down and write while I have the thought well in mind.

Yes, I do have a suggestion! You asked for it, and here it is. You're never going to be equal to the problem of handling Jill (whether she is a big problem or a little one) until you get over this obsession of being so old! To hear you talk, one might gather you were among the authors of the Great Books instead of the students. True, there is a gap between your age and Jill's, but, by letting yourself get carried away with the thought of being so old, are you not widening the gap rather than bridging it? Can you not agree that age is a matter of feeling, not years?

I could not feel more strongly about this. Let me cite the example that has firmly convinced me that it is true. I don't know if you have heard me mention her name, but I have worked at the university for two years with Mrs. Lucile Weatherly, secretary to the dean of the business school. I don't know Lucile's exact age (somewhere this or that side of fifty), but, when you know Lucile, it doesn't matter. She seems young.

It is not her appearance or any part of her physical makeup. It seems to be the state of her mind. While her years of experience have added to her wisdom, she is always receptive to a new idea. Her purposeful way of living each day to its utmost would never suggest the bitterness with which she might have been engulfed when her husband suddenly died eleven months after their marriage in 1927. Having lived these years alone, without a husband or children, should make her feel very old indeed. Yet she seems to look forward to tomorrow and the next day with as much vitality and anticipation as a sixteen-year-old. Maybe she even feels a creaky joint or two or three now and then, but, after all, if it isn't one thing, it's another. And it used to be skinned knees.

Though I am yet young in years and relatively inexperienced, knowing Lucile has made me realize that young is not a twenty-one-inch waist, a wrinkle-free face, or jet-black hair without any springs of gray. Young is how you feel, and how you feel can be largely determined by how you make up your mind and decide to feel.

You've been blaming your trouble with Jill on the notion that you are too old to handle her. Why not try to dispose of this obstacle, that is, this excuse. Then maybe you can get down to the real problem, whatever it may be. Now you may not agree with all this, but this is the trouble as I see it, and I think I'm far enough removed from the scene to be objective.

I know you're not given to playing jukeboxes, Mother dear, but, at the earliest opportunity, it will be worth your nickel to hear a new song called "When You're Young At Heart." Play it now because I think you'll like it.

I love you,
Beverly

Bobby

I NTROSPECTION WAS NOT MY SISTER'S long suit. Beverly's philosophy of life seemed to be, "Take on whatever needs to be done with a happy heart, and do your best. The rest will fall in line." She was confident, rarely second-guessing her decisions or actions. Beverly's philosophy was severely tested when her first child, Bobby, died in an accident. Mother spared me the tragic news, thinking death should not be in my vocabulary during my formative years. When Mother received word of Bobby's death, she locked herself in her bedroom, where I was not allowed. She and Daddy left for Missouri the next day, leaving me with the Bumpers.

My understanding of our family tragedy is as follows. Soon after Beverly and Bob were married, she became pregnant, and Bob Taylor Jr. was born. By the time of Bobby's second birthday, Bob was called to serve in the Korean War and stationed overseas. He insisted that Beverly and the baby live with his parents in Columbia, Missouri. The Taylors lived on an acreage near the edge of town.

One midsummer evening, the Taylors and Beverly strolled out with Bobby to watch the hired help load some equipment behind their tractor. Naturally, he was enamored with the tractor, so the man offered to give him a ride. After he placed Bobby in the seat, he told him to sit still while he hooked up a trailer.

Though Bobby stayed seated, he swung his foot and accidentally hit the gearshift knob. The tractor kicked into gear and lurched forward. The momentum knocked Bobby's tiny body backward out of the seat, and the trailer ran over him as his mother and grandparents stood helpless nearby. Bobby died from his injuries the next day. The family delayed the funeral until Bob returned on emergency leave from the war zone.

Beverly and Bob talked through their loss for a week. Then they never mentioned it again. She soon became pregnant with their second son, Blane. In the next three years, their daughters, Gail and Nancy, were born. The Taylor family was complete.

When they were preteens, Gail and Nancy, during a visit at their Grandmother Taylor's house, noticed a picture on the dresser of a cute baby boy.

"Who is he?" they asked.

"Oh, that's your brother," their grandmother replied.

"It sure doesn't look like Blane to me," Gail said while holding the photo up to her face for close inspection.

Their grandmother spoke, "It's not Blane. It's little Bobby. He died before you were born."

This was the first they knew of their brother. It wasn't until my mid-thirties that Beverly said anything to me about the accident. I learned she didn't mention a word of the tragedy even to her closest friends, which surprised me. I envisioned her sharing much more with them than she did with me.

Pill Hill

1957

DURING THE SUMMER BEFORE I started the sixth grade, Daddy heard about a good opportunity on a nearby house. While Mother had never mentioned a hankering for a new house, Daddy knew a deal when he saw it, and he was quietly proud of his ability to move us up.

1416 Sunrise Lane was located halfway up or down the main hill in the Norris Hills Addition. It was affectionately called "Pill Hill" because at least six doctors and their families lived there. Long before it was developed, P.A. Norris had had elm trees planted in double rows where streets would eventually run between them. It was a shame, years later, when the Dutch elm disease wiped out much of the shade his foresight had provided.

Our new house was twice the size of the one on Eighth Street. It was built on a cement slab and had central heat and air. The tile floor in the kitchen and den furnished a level place for a game of jacks and gave cool relief to my bare feet on hot summer afternoons.

Though I appreciated my own bedroom, it was anything but warm and inviting. Any closed door bothered Frances because she couldn't see what was going on behind it, so the house rule was that my bedroom door must remain open. My door had a knocker and bell, which was unusual for an interior door. I never used them because I could never shut it. Twin beds lined the walls. A four-foot square, pink, pine box was between them, holding extra quilts and blankets. The top served as a nightstand. The slate gray walls were in contrast to the medium blue-polished cotton café curtains. Because the windows were on the east, it was necessary to pull the shades to cut early morning light. During my mother's blue light phase, the overhead light held a blue bulb, which, with the dark walls, gave the room an ultra-ray feel. When my mother would turn on the light to wake me up, the irritation of that light was akin to fingernails scratching a chalkboard.

Even though Clifford's work took him away from home, it gave him great satisfaction to have such a nice house on a quarter-acre lot within a long stone's throw from the country club golf course. Mother may have squawked about the move. I really don't remember. I do know she was in charge of all basic maintenance projects.

Daddy wasn't handy. I probably didn't see him mow the lawn more than a couple of times. In fairness, Daddy did lift a finger while he was home by fixing the coffee and bringing in the paper every morning, taking out the trash, and quietly washing the dishes after dinner.

When he was in town, golf was his favorite pastime. Then he would get into a card game over a drink at the club. Mother fretted, stewed, and became easily agitated over the magnitude of household responsibilities that fell on her shoulders during his frequent absences as well as when he was home and enjoying himself.

"Don't come in here with that sad face looking hungry. I told you we are waiting for Clifford to come home from the club. You should have taken me up on the celery I offered you before I put the chicken tetrazzini in the oven," she said.

I turned back to the front bedroom to read. The next thing I knew, the news was over. Mother turned off the television, turned on the kitchen overhead light, and dropped the lid from the pan of Brussels sprouts, which she knew I would not touch, on the countertop to add a bit more water. Her search for matches was audible. I walked into the kitchen as Mother finished lighting a cigarette. She pursed her bottom lip out for that first, most satisfying exhale and started in when she saw me.

"Clifford Byrne is still out at the club enjoying himself, and I've got a mind to go ahead and dish up the plates. He doesn't think for a minute that you are hungry. We don't see him for six weeks, and all he does is hang out every evening with those good old boys at the club. He expects me to keep this kitchen open when I'm tired from all I do around here and ready to go to bed. He does not help me one whit."

She smashed out the cigarette in the ashtray I had made in art class the year before.

The headlights from Daddy's car hit the wall. The slam of the car door followed. He couldn't miss the fury in her eyes when he came in the back door.

"Oh, honey, I'm sorry," he said. "I didn't think you'd wait dinner on me. Go sit down, and let me fix you a little drink. Jill, how 'bout a short Coke before we eat?"

They sat in the living room for ten minutes while he told her some jokes he heard earlier around the card table. I waited in the den until all was forgiven. Dinner was served at eight thirty sharp.

"IN CASE MY daddy is running late, save us a place tonight," I said.

"Sure," Jane replied as we separated on the walk home from Willard. She continued north one more block over on Northcrest Drive. I turned east down the hill on Sunrise Lane.

I was going to the Campfire Girls Annual Father-Daughter Banquet at the college student union. Last night, Mother had put the finishing touches on my decorated shoebox that would hold our dinner. In hopes of winning "best box," I agreed with her idea to cover the whole thing in tinfoil instead of the crepe paper we used last year. My part was to cut out and decorate red and pink construction paper hearts. The first thing I noticed when I walked in the house was my box on the kitchen table. Mother had redecorated it.

"What happened to the hearts I colored last night?" I asked.

"You said you wanted to win, so I cut this paper chain of Campfire Girls to give it more punch. I thought you could color their hats and uniforms if you wanted," she replied.

Mother was peeling carrots at the kitchen sink to go with the tuna fish sandwiches already wrapped in wax paper.

"By the way," she said over her shoulder, "Cliff got a call and took off for central Arkansas not long after you left for school. I told him you would understand. Besides, Uel is willing to fill in for him tonight. Ellen is contributing banana cream pie for your dessert, so get rid of that bottom lip."

We arrived before Jane and her father, so we saved them a place instead. Directly across from Uel and me was Lynn's dad, Dr. Ramsay, a rather stern man who sat silently between Lynn and Barbara, whose father was out of town. While Barbara's and my dad were often out of town, Lynn's dad missed his share of events, too, because of being called into emergency surgery.

Lynn's box had held her older brother's Converse high-top sneakers, so it easily held dinner for three. Already an accomplished perfectionist, Lynn had decorated her box in patriotic colors and spelled out the Campfire motto of "Wo-He-Lo" with pipe cleaners that sparkled with red and blue glitter. That explained those shiny flecks on her navy vest uniform, which was covered with various beads representing awards of merit she had earned. The thirteen beads sewn on my vest paled by comparison. Barbara's bead count fell somewhere in the middle.

After dinner, we pushed all the tables back so there was plenty of room to do the Hokey-Pokey more than once while the judges deliberated over the now-empty boxes.

Uel said, "Jill, we need to go on and leave a little early. I know they haven't announced the winner yet, but I promised Janie I would be home in time to tuck her in bed."

"Okay, I'm ready," I said. "Let me ask Jane to call and tell me who wins best box."

"All right," Uel said. "I'll go get the car and pick you up at the door. Don't forget your box. Ellen said to be sure and get home with the dessert plate."

I brushed my teeth. I was crawling into bed when the phone rang. Changing direction, I rushed in the kitchen to answer.

After I hung up, Mother called from the den, "Who won?"

"Lynn," I said. "I guess all that glitter did it."

Longhorn

1958–1968

OON AFTER WE MOVED TO Sunrise Lane, I learned that Judy Norris would be moving in behind us. Judy, who I would come to call "Norris," was a granddaughter of P. A. Norris. Her family lived on the other side of town, and she attended Washington, the rival elementary school. We Willard girls knew the Washington girls to be conceited, and we considered Judy to be the most conceited of the bunch. Prior to her father's untimely death in a traffic accident, she had lived in a large house, so now, while the Byrnes were moving up, Judy's mom was scaling down.

By the beginning of the school year, including Barbara and Lynn, there were six of us classmates living in Norris Hills. Our initial reluctance to include Judy was short-lived. She turned out to be much less conceited than we expected. Much to our surprise, she was smart in school. She was a fast runner, and she could swim like a fish. Best of all, she had her very own horse, Sadie.

I credit Norris for encouraging, actually insisting, that I attend Camp Longhorn with her. Norris and her cousins were the first from Ada to attend the camp. Counting Barbara and Lynn, the Norris cousins led close to twenty Ada kids to that camp. Camp Longhorn was a residential summer camp for kids aged eight to sixteen. Located in the Texas Hill Country, it was sixty miles northwest of Austin on the shore of Inks Lake. A former Olympic swimmer and Texas University swim coach, Tex Robertson and his wife, Pat, founded Camp Longhorn for Boys in 1939. Eleven years later, they started Camp Longhorn for Girls.

Camp Longhorn operated on the merit system. Campers earned merits for good deeds each day and could save them year to year or spend them in the merit store, which was filled with child-pleasing items, like orange nightshirts, goo goo hats, stuffed longhorns, lanyards, record albums, and even small television sets. In my days there, the value of a merit equaled about a dime. Longhorn also had a policy that each camper had to earn the privilege of being invited back to camp. Sometime during the last ten days of a term (a typical term was four weeks), campers received word whether they would be invited to return or not. Most got this news early in the ten-day period. A few received their invites on the last day. Fewer still did not receive anything at all.

Until the sixth grade, I reluctantly refused to join them because of my deadly fear of getting the shots needed for the camping experience. One tetanus shot and a series of three typhoid immunizations were required. As much as I secretly aspired to be a Longhorn girl, I simply lacked the courage to meet those enrollment requirements.

All that changed when I won the grand prize at the camp carnival held in the spring at Trigg's house. (Trigg was Norris' cousin.) I was told that, if I would sign up for camp right then, I could trade in the grand prize, a rifle I did not want, for its value in merits. The prospect of starting out with over two hundred merits before I even arrived at Longhorn spurred me to decide to endure the shots for the greater good. I was hooked. I began to dream of walking arm in arm with my friends at camp singing, "Oh, when a Longhorn girl walks down the street …"

Quite a few Longhorn counselors were former campers who had continued their camping interest and possessed leadership ability. Most Camp Longhorn's counselors were selected from among college students and young adults after a personal interview. A few junior counselors were culled from the most promising older (high school-aged) campers and trained under close supervision of senior counselors and camp directors.

Camp Longhorn's promotional material spoke of the "magic constantly created between campers, counselors, and staff, who return year after year." For eleven summers, from 1958 through 1968, I was part of that magic. I was initially a camper. Then I was a junior counselor. Finally, I was a senior counselor.

I was a model first-time camper in 1958. When I arrived, much about the place was rustic. The bull nettle stickers were everywhere. If we went outside the cabin without shoes, we received a demerit as well as stinging welts on our feet. In those early years, everyone pitched in to put down St. Augustine grass sod. Years later, our efforts produced a "field of green." The grass was so lush that my feet disappeared in it. It was no longer necessary to wear shoes anywhere around. The drinking fountain, "Old Faceful," bubbled the best water on earth. Wasting water earned a demerit.

My second summer, however, was a disaster. When it came to acting up, I found camp to be a much safer place than home. Staff members at Camp Longhorn worked diligently to provide close supervision of all campers, so I considered escapes, even in the early morning hours, to be a coup. I sometimes left my bunk long after lights out and walked around camp in the dark. On full-moon nights, I sat on the back deck of our floating cabin and watched the skittering light on the water. I wallowed in feeling alone and not good enough.

The third summer went much better. I had a counselor, Lou, who made an effort to really listen to me. My response to this personal attention gave me incentive to curb my nocturnal wandering.

The summer of 1961, my Wrangler year and my first year in a two-year training to become a junior counselor, was my most rebellious. After the senior staff completed the late-night second head count, I left the cabin, heading for the swim bay diving board or the archery range. Once, when I was too tired to rise and shine the next morning, the counselors resorted to flipping my mattress on my top bunk with me still in it.

That summer, we had some free nights away from camp at the local drive-in theater. By the time we filed off the camp bus and made a beeline for the concession stand, the challenge of an eating contest was underway. I felt a tremendous sense of accomplishment when I knocked down three or four barbecue sandwiches with mayo and relish, a couple bags of chips, a hot fudge sundae, and six doughnuts. Then I would wash it all down with an extra large Coke. I won every food eating competition we had that summer. While the pounds packed on, it never occurred to me to purge like the girls from Wichita Falls did when they lost.

On the flip side of earning merits for exemplary behavior, demerits were handed out for rules infractions. In any twenty-four hour period, acquiring five demerits garnered the camper some intense one-on-one time with Tex, the owner. That summer, he helped me see the errors of my ways twice. None of my friends spent this kind of time with Tex.

"WAIT FOR ME over by Trigger's tree. I'll be back in a minute," Tex said.

Tex strode off to the swim bay, leaving me anxiously anticipating his return. Third-period swimming was wrapping up. All I could see of Tex in the distance was the white pith helmet he wore. He strolled along the crowd of counselors near the shoreline and walked past the swimmers lined up for eardrops. He stopped for a brief word with Bob Hudson, the camp director for the girls. I picked blade after blade of St. Augustine grass to chew on. Tex circled the tennis courts, stooped to pick up paper trash, and finally settled beside a nervous me.

"Didn't we have this same talk just last week?" Tex asked as he removed his headgear and ran his fingers through his wavy, salt-and-pepper hair.

The leathery squint lines around his cool, blue eyes were proof of the damage my mother drilled into me of too much sun exposure over the years.

He growled, "How did this happen again?"

I began at the beginning. "Two were cabin demerits. One was because we laughed after lights out. The other was because we missed a cobweb before inspection yesterday."

"And the other three?" he asked.

"I forgot to wear my hat when I went to pick up cabin refreshments, and I was late to canoeing because my bathing suit was still wet and too hard to get into," I said.

"And?" he asked.

"I accidentally spilled my milk in the chow hall," I said.

"I don't know what has gotten into you, Jill. As a fourth-year camper and in your first year of the Wrangler program, I expect you to be setting an example of responsibility instead of going around willy-nilly and unfocused. Do you know this will affect your early bird invitation to return to camp next year?" he asked.

"Yes, sir," I said.

"You don't want me to call your parents, do you? What do you have to say for yourself?" he asked.

My watery eyes stopped short of overflowing.

I said, "I couldn't believe I got five demerits the first time. You're not the only one shocked that it happened twice."

"Then go blow your nose and hustle over to the chow hall so you can have lunch with the other food servers in your cabin," he instructed me.

"Okay," I said. "Thank you, sir."

I took off running across the baseball field and never looked back.

On the last day of camp, I received my invitation to return the following summer. Though relieved to be accepted, I was crushed that all those demerits really had impacted the delayed invitation. I marched to the merit store and spent every last merit I had accumulated in my account, vowing to myself in humiliation that I would not return.

The last night of every term seemed to provoke emotions in campers about memories and love for their times at camp. That night, while singing the camp song, I became overwhelmed with remorse for my misbehavior over the last month and began sobbing uncontrollably. Years before, I had willed myself to never cry. Once that secret code was broken, I was beyond help. I cried for every recent act of disobedience I had committed. I cried harder for every hurt I had silently endured through my entire junior high career. Because mental health issues were not actively addressed in the 1950s, the staff did what they could to console me. Not even putting my head under a running faucet could stop my torrent of tears. As a last resort, the staff sedated me and put me to bed. The next morning, I awoke in an empty cabin. My shame for losing control was deep. The fear it could happen again grew and stayed with me long after one might expect.

Once on the bus leaving for home, I was overcome with remorse for showing such weakness the night before and for every disobedient thing I had done during the whole term. I was clearly aware I had blown my chance of becoming a junior counselor.

My regret did not dissipate with time. Three weeks later, I awoke one morning and knew that, more than anything, I wanted to turn it around. There was only one way to do this. I would return to Longhorn on the next visitors' day, apologize to the camp directors, and pledge to give my best the following year.

Neither of my parents had any inkling of my difficulties at camp the month before, but my mother overheard my part of the phone conversation with Daddy.

I asked, "If you're coming home at the end of next week, will you please drive me down to Longhorn for Visitors' Day?"

He said, "We'll see."

I knew that meant there was a good chance he would make it happen. Without my saying it, he knew it must be important for me to ask him for something this big. Begging him to take me to the Dairy Queen after dinner was one thing. But Daddy drove at least fifty thousand miles a year. Now I was asking him to drive close to another thousand over the weekend on his time off.

When we hung up the phone, Mother went into a tirade.

"That is the most ridiculous and selfish thing I've ever heard of. Clifford Byrne is not about to drive you off to Texas for anything. Don't think for a minute that I'm going to let that happen."

All through the next week, I never gave up believing that my daddy would come through.

He had said, "We'll see."

I planned what to wear and rehearsed what I would say at camp. I was packed when Daddy pulled in the driveway after three o'clock on Friday afternoon.

When Mother realized that Daddy was going to drive me to Longhorn, she launched in.

"Cliff, it makes absolutely no sense for you to come in here tired from being on the road for three weeks and let Jill get away with thinking about nobody but herself. She's not lifted a finger to help me all week. I even had to threaten her with no swimming at the club if she didn't make her bed."

Without my revealing why it was important, Daddy sensed it was. Amid my mother's comments of disgust, the two of us were on the road within the hour. Daddy got a speeding ticket outside Waco. We checked into a motel after eleven o'clock that night.

Up early the next morning, we arrived at the camp by ten o'clock. Daddy told me to take care of whatever I needed to do. He was content to tour himself around in the meantime.

I went to both directors separately and apologized for all the nights I left the cabin after lights out to roam the camp and sit on the high dive at the swim bay until the wee hours. I was sorry they had to start locking the cabin from the outside to assure my safety. Admitting I was a poor sailor, I had not meant to capsize the boat when all of us aboard were fully clothed. Also, I knew it was wrong to refuse to come down from the top of the tree and accept it when I finally received my invitation back to camp. These were among the issues I needed to address. Both directors agreed they would like to see me turn it around the next year.

My mission was accomplished. Daddy and I were back in Ada before midnight. Daddy's unquestioning assistance turned out to be a cornerstone in my young life.

By the end of January, I had compiled a list of nearly a dozen things I would need to do differently at camp, such as get out of bed before they turned over my mattress. I referred to the list until I memorized it as my personal mantra.

I came back to Longhorn the following year as a Wrangler Chief, the term applied to those in their second year of junior counselor training. Forty-five of us vied for fifteen positions. Unlike the invitation process for the rest of the camp, we were graded and evaluated throughout the term. We were tested at the conclusion of formal classes in counselor concepts and techniques. The concept of initiative and how to take it seemed to make the greatest impression on me. The competition and pressure was intense all month. I gave it all I had every day, and I made a huge point not to cry that last night of the term.

And I made it! I was one of the fifteen selected.

Time on Her Hands

1958

WITH DADDY GONE ON ASSIGNMENTS for long periods, Mother literally had a lot of time on her hands. Unlike her sisters who sat and knitted, crocheted, quilted, or did embroidery, sewing was the only sort of handwork Mother pursued. Between projects though, she stayed busy, mostly in the singular pursuits of crossword puzzles, cryptograms, solitaire, and lots of reading. Occasionally, she and Thena got into marathon Scrabble games that would stretch on for five or six hours at a time. Mother's intense competitiveness at the bridge table was legendary. However, she had almost hung up her cards because the doctor said her blood pressure was out of sight. I was glad for that because I hated all the smoke when they played at our house and I hated having to tag along when they played at night.

It wasn't uncommon to come home from school and see wafts of layered smoke still floating around Mother's chair by the window. It signaled what she had been doing while I had been at school. Along with the ashes, cigarette butts with varying amounts of lipstick filled the turquoise, ceramic ashtray Thena had given her for Christmas the year before. The contents were covering the black Japanese writing I knew was on the bottom. On the ottoman was her current page-turner, *The Eagles Gather* by Taylor Caldwell. Mother always said there was a generational epic book there in Ada for Taylor Caldwell to write if she would have just come there and researched the history of the Norris family and the bank they owned.

Whenever we got the word that Daddy was coming home for a few days, or maybe a week, my mother went into a frenzy. She put her hair in pin curls and began to clean like no tomorrow, which I found unsettling.

"Surely it's not too much to ask for you to scoot out in the back-yard and gather the clothes off the line. It's a crying shame no one puts out any effort to help me around here," she complained.

When my mother said "no one," she meant me. She wasn't talking about Daddy because he had been leasing minerals for Gulf Oil up in Wyoming since the week before school started. And Beverly was long gone, raising her own family in Dallas.

Mother was right. I didn't help out much. When there was work to be done, she got so into the project that my meager efforts were soon dashed when her voice rang out.

"Jill, how many times must I tell you to move all the dining chairs out of here first instead of you trying to run the sweeper around them?"

"Jill, your dusting missed a spot on the windowsill here above the piano."

'Jill, that is no way to peel a carrot. Put that knife down. Get out of this kitchen before somebody gets hurt, and it's not going to be me."

Basic life skills escaped me as I left this scene of intensity. I slipped away with a nickel for a package of M&Ms at a nearby drugstore. (It is fair to say that I have learned to clean a sink with lots of Babo to her satisfaction.)

I dragged out my return from the store, walking slowly to let each M&M melt individually. I started with the brown ones and then went onto the tan, orange, red, and yellow. I finally got to my favorite green ones as I came back down the driveway. I opened the door in the car-port.

"Yoo-hoo! Where are you?" I sang out.

My mother sang back, "I'm in the bathroom putting on my face. Grab a spoon, and stir those carrots on the right burner. I'll be out in a minute."

It was second nature for me to be a bit tentative when stirring any-thing for her, but, fortunately, before I could inflict any damage on the carrots, I heard the click of her high heels as she came down the hall into the kitchen. She was adjusting her right earring.

"Let me do that. Watch out! You are letting the lid drip water on the counter I just cleaned. Why don't you go back, get out of those blue jeans, and put on something presentable?" she asked.

When I returned, the kitchen was empty. I peeked in the living room to find Mother standing in the window, where she always waited for Daddy to turn in. He wasn't here yet. I couldn't tell if she was looking at anything. She was thinking too hard to notice that I was even in the room. She cupped her left elbow in her right hand as the smoke from her Winston snaked toward the ceiling. I jumped when she twirled around. Her full skirt swished as she moved.

"Maybe you should take some private speech lessons. You don't know the first thing about elocution," she remarked.

Again, Mother was right. But I did know enough to stay away from big trees when there was lightning.

Junior High

1958

I REMEMBER THE DRESS I WORE when my mother took me to enroll in the seventh grade. Over the weekend, she had finished making this low-waisted white dress with faint horizontal stripes of pastel blue and green. A black velvet ribbon wove through the eyelet sewn on the low waist and was tied in a bow off to the left side.

My mother had honed her sewing skills well during my last four years at Willard Elementary. My red squaw dress with gold rickrack was possibly the most memorable. Now we were entering the big time, junior high school. When she got on a fabric high, it was best for me to stay out of her way.

Occasionally, my mother would say, "Jill, do you think four or three buttons look better on this bodice?"

If I said four, she would settle for three. She had given me a similar choice regarding which side to tie the black velvet ribbon on. You guessed it. I preferred the right.

When it got down to it, I didn't care how many buttons or what side the bow was on, I relied heavily on her opinion of what was cute. But never guessing right did undermine my fashion confidence

To hear my mother talk, I was one of the most unappreciative daughters who ever walked the face of the earth. Fittings were hell for both of us. They could often end abruptly with her furious and fed up with my lack of cooperation to silently stand still indefinitely. Notice I said "silently." That meant sighing was unacceptable.

"Jill, put down that book and get yourself in here. I am worn to a frazzle, and I can't do another thing on this dress until I see how the plaid on the bodice lines up with the skirt," she would say.

I tossed my book aside, got up grudgingly from the couch, and, like a convict heading to the gallows, trudged back to the full-length mirror in Daddy's bedroom.

"Am I imposing on you? Stand still here in front of the mirror while I make sure the fabric matches up. For the life of me, you are not walking out of the house wearing this dress with shoddy, unmatched seams," she said.

"Ow!" I interjected.

"I told you the bodice is only pinned together," she said. "Keep your arms up and wait while I go get the yardstick. Then I'll help you ease the bodice down."

"It's too tight," I said.

"Suck it in, and stop your whining," she said.

Later that night, sound asleep in bed, I was awakened with, "Jill, get up out of bed and come back here one more time. I'm almost finished, so pull yourself together and act enthused just once."

I slipped out of bed and staggered down the hall. This time, I was like a drunken sailor rather than a convict. Mother had been sewing since I had gone to bed.

"Okay, all that's left is the hem," she said. "Stand up straight. When I say, you turn slowly to your right. Hand me the yardstick on the dresser."

Sitting on the floor, Mother measured, pinned, and remeasured while my partially suppressed sigh escaped.

She said, "I don't want to hear a peep out of you. Stand still. I did not tell you to turn."

Mother shifted positions. Her back was no longer facing the mirror.

"Now look what happened here!" she exclaimed. "Stand evenly. This whole hem on the left side is catawampus. I have had it up to here." She struck the air above her head. "You know, this may be the very last dress I ever make for you."

I heard Mother folding up the sewing machine in the den. We met in the hall.

"Will you please unzip me?" I whispered.

"Since you found your manners, yes, I will, if you turn around," she said.

Starting junior high meant new teachers and many more students than just the Willard crowd. My mother and I arrived early and picked up my schedule. Mother visited with a few teachers while I selected a locker. A bunch of my friends were coming en masse later in the morning, so I escaped the embarrassment of enrolling with my mother. We both accepted compliments on my cute, new dress.

With enrollment over, we went to town and celebrated with a cherry Coke at a drugstore fountain. Looking around afterward, she allowed me to pick out my first lipstick, pink ice. From there we jaywalked to the shoe store.

She told Sonny, "Jill needs a sensible black pump with a heel for Sunday."

That was it. I had come of age, and I hadn't even had to whine or beg for a thing.

Never being sure of what to expect left me on hyperalert and overprepared for her negative response. And that response didn't come the day I enrolled in junior high. It was just a nice day.

Upon entering junior high, certain members of our class were chosen for an experimental accelerated program. At year's end, the program was abandoned, possibly due to the elitist attitudes that its members assumed. Participants were selected on the recommendation of the sixth-grade teachers from elementary school.

I strongly believe each student's ability to thrive during a school year is directly related to the quality of the relationship that exists between the teacher and each student. My sixth-grade year was no exception.

Mrs. Edna K. Wallace probably thought she was a nice, perfectly normal adult. To me, she was the epitome of a battle-axe. I have no recollection of her appearing to enjoy one moment of time spent in the classroom. In fact, my most vivid memory is of her waving a yardstick in my face while trying to extract an answer from me regarding the top three exports from the Belgian Congo. My concentration was limited on the three inches separating my nose from the end of the yardstick. The exports were truly continents away from what I viewed as personally important.

Essentially, Mrs. Wallace and I didn't like each other very much, and hence she chose not to recommend me for the accelerated program the following year.

Mrs. Wallace's revenge ended when I earned straight As in the first grading period. I was then abruptly transferred into the accelerated English class, which a formidable woman, Mrs. Edith Hudson, taught. She directed me to a chair and continued with her pep talk already in progress.

Her deep voice thundered, "You people in this class think you are so superior. Well, I want to know. Superior in what?"

Now Mrs. Hudson, a former basketball player, was taller than anyone in the class. She had olive skin and the bluest deep-set eyes I had ever seen. When her eyes locked hard with a student who was out of line, she could see all the way to his or her soul. He or she had nowhere to hide. After she stared down every uppity pupil, she gently welcomed me to the class. From that day until her final one a few years ago, she had my total respect.

Mrs. Hudson was inarguably outspoken and entertaining whether sharing the merits and works of Edgar Allen Poe or allowing us to divert her into a class period of storytelling. Her love of poetry was contagious. There were few dry eyes and lots of sniffles at the conclusion of her reading our class favorite, "Little Boy Blue." I felt safe and protected in her presence, even as she raised her intensity to stare down any classmate who dared to misbehave. Many from our class remained her loyal followers by celebrating her birthday long after our names were removed from her roll book.

Mrs. Hudson's sponsorship of the yearbook and "Blue Jay Chatter" newspaper steered me into journalism classes during the last two years of junior high. With no visible writing skills, my contribution was primarily limited to the collage pages of the yearbook, which sometimes meant staying after school to meet a deadline. On those occasions, Mrs. Hudson drove me home. As the years went by, I always knew, if needed, Mrs. Hudson would give me a ride home even if I stayed late in high school. Both the junior and senior highs shared a campus.

Once during my junior year when I asked her for a ride, Mrs. Hudson said, "Sure, but I can't leave the building until four thirty today. I need some Christmas ribbon, so why don't you take my car downtown and get some. I'll be ready to go when you get back."

As I carefully put the car in reverse, I swelled with pride that Mrs. Hudson trusted me to drive her new Cadillac, which was vast in contrast to my mother's reluctance to let me drive her Impala.

My mother never liked Mrs. Hudson.

One day, as I opened the front door after school, Mother called from the kitchen, "Who brought you home?"

I replied, "I caught a ride with Mrs. Hudson."

This garnered an instant "harrumph." Mother didn't even look up from her dummy hands of bridge sprawled across the kitchen table. I could tell she disliked anyone who liked me.

Years later, I told Mrs. Hudson of my struggles with depression. She said she knew that my mother was overly strict, but she hadn't realized the depth of my emotional pain. She thought I was simply starved for a kind word and a pat on the back.

My daddy received calls from an oil company to buy leases that took him to Bismarck, North Dakota; Odessa, Texas; Russellville, Arkansas; Cheyenne, Wyoming; Charleston, West Virginia; and Limon, Colorado, to name a few destinations. Before dawn on Monday mornings, he set off for far points with his Samsonite suitcase, dop kit, seven freshly ironed shirts, coat, hat, and a carton of Camels.

Being a naturally early riser, he made the coffee and downed a quick cup before he left. If I heard him, I got up to tell him goodbye. I hated to see him leave, never knowing exactly when he would be back home. Yet I knew he was providing a living for us, and I was proud of the frequency of calls wanting his services. There was a certain amount of secrecy that went with this line of work. Oil companies competed for leases in hot areas, so it was important not to divulge his whereabouts to others.

When my daddy began driving America, the interstate system was not in place. Speed limits of sixty miles per hour were enforced. As he drove two-lane roads, waiting for an opportunity to pass, he rested his left arm on the rolled-down window. Over time, his left arm became permanently two shades darker than his right. His time on the road was greatly reduced with the development of the interstates. With his keen sense of direction, I never knew him to get lost.

When my daddy came home, he usually stayed about a week. During the fall, he tried to take an in-state assignment or coincide his trips home with the Sooners football games. One summer, I asked him if he would take me to Dallas so I could stay with Beverly, Bob, and the kids.

"Well, I guess we could work that out. I need to see an old boy about a lease near Waupaunuka on the way. Let's get an early start in the morning," he said.

"If we leave by eight, we should be there by just after noon," I thought. "I'll dress up so Beverly and I can go shopping right after lunch."

Up at six o'clock in the morning to pack, I wore a new sleeveless gray, green, and pink print sheath that my mother had made for me the week before. The outfit was set off with a wide, white, patent leather belt and white flats with pointy toes. Even in the summertime, I had to wear hose with flats, and the shoes still hurt my feet.

Two hours later, we promptly backed out of the driveway.

"Wave to your mother," Daddy said as we headed up the hill.

Mother stood in the living room window as Daddy pulled away.

After driving a while, Daddy said, "Now that turnoff is up here somewhere on the left. Help me look for it."

"But, Daddy, that's not the way to Waupaunuka," I argued.

"I know, Jill," he said. "But I ran into Jim Armstrong at the post office last night, and he asked me to stop by and see if old man Jennings would talk to his oldest son's widow about signing that lease over in Atoka County."

"But, Daddy, we're gonna be late," I said.

"I know, Jill," he said. "But we'll hurry."

The blacktop lasted about a mile after we turned off the highway. I turned around to watch the dust billowing behind us.

"Here comes an old pickup. Better roll up your window, Jill. He's going pretty fast," he said.

Daddy read his directions from the back of an envelope, "Right at the four-way stop. Left after the one-lane bridge. Three more miles to the white house at the end of the road."

As we slowed to a stop near a discarded bathtub by the gate, a dirty, spotted white dog ran barking to the fence.

"Nobody's home, Daddy." I said, hoping he would agree so we would get out of there.

"I'll go see, Jill. You stay in the car," he said.

The mangy dog's bark intensified into a low growl as my daddy stepped through the gate.

"Oh, please don't bite him," I said. "I don't know what I'll do if my daddy doesn't come back."

A man yelled, "Shooooo, Spike! Get back." A figure appeared on the porch. "Whatcha want?"

My daddy approached the house with his straw hat in one hand and his tattered briefcase in the other. I couldn't hear what they were saying, but they moved into the house in a couple of minutes. Thankfully, I had brought a book with me, though it was hard to concentrate in this heat. My hose bunched at the knee and ankle, and it was next to impossible to adjust them because I was so sweaty and all. It also didn't help that the back of my new dress was stuck to the plastic upholstery. And this was just the first stop.

I leaned over to use the rearview mirror. All the kids I knew would swivel it, but Mother had warned me that there was no good reason to fiddle with the mirror.

"Maybe this was a good time to put a little Clearasil on my chin where I'm breaking out," I thought.

Finally, Daddy appeared at the door. The other guy followed him out on the porch and stood with his hands wrapped around his suspenders.

"Come on, Daddy," I pleaded silently. "Don't stand there. You've talked long enough. I'm hot out here."

"Sorry that took so long, JB," Daddy said as he threw his briefcase in the backseat, started the car, and adjusted the air-conditioner to its coldest blast.

"Can we stop at the next Dairy Queen we see for a cherry Coke?"

I asked. I could see my lunch plans in Dallas evaporate along with the mirage of water on the road ahead.

The worst thing about riding with my daddy was that I never knew just how long it would take. The best thing was that it was never boring because he rarely went the same way twice, which whetted my spirit of adventure.

I enjoyed looking out the window as much as reading in the car, which were both silent activities. Neither my daddy nor I chatted when we traveled together. Over the miles, I developed a comfort with silence. Even today, I enjoy ruminating on the lives of those I drive by, wondering which ones made their beds that morning, which ones have health problems, or which ones will eat alone tonight.

A Part of the Crowd

1958–1959

THE BASIC DICHOTOMY OF JUNIOR high was fitting in and standing out. A piece of fitting in was secured for me when I was finally allowed to wear penny loafers instead of saddle oxfords with my bobby sox. I, too, carried a black bucket purse that, without close inspection, appeared identical to any other junior high girl's.

When I think about the social order of the girls in my class, I don't have a sense there was an in crowd. Maybe it was because I felt I was in the group, which consisted of roughly twenty-five girls. Basically, we ruled by consensus with a lot of fluidity of best friendships within our circle. It is possible I may have been too immature to realize I was on the fringe and didn't know it. Whatever the case, I felt included enough. My stress was more about balancing my social opportunities with my mother's seemingly constant state of disapproval regarding my desire to fit in.

A sign you had made the in crowd came when friends toilet-papered your house and yard. While the art or act of papering did not begin or end with our class, we upheld the tradition better than most back before one paid a premium for toilet paper. When I say "we," please know I was only on the periphery of this activity a couple of times. I lived in holy fear of my house being papered in turn. There were many motives involved in the selection of who was papered and who was spared. On plenty of weekend nights, I slept in the living room to guard our yard from the actualization of rumors. My mother would not have rolled with it had we been papered. I felt great relief that no threats of papering were ever carried out at our home on Sunrise Lane.

The ramifications of standing out were more visibly symptomatic of my difficulties at home. What better way to celebrate a holiday in the seventh grade than for my mother to decide to make me a theme dress. Using a shirtwaist pattern, she saw that I sported a black-and-white striped, polished cotton dress with six individually decorated orange felt pumpkins placed just above the hemline. In February, the same pattern was converted to sequined white and pink valentines on solid red, polished cotton fabric. She had both two-inch wide belts covered with matching fabric and then cinched them up as much as she could to accentuate my narrow waist. No one would ever say Frances Byrne did not do her best to help her midlife baby stand out.

My mother also poured herself into every election campaign I entered. Whether class office, student council, or pep club election, not only did my posters stand out for their clever sayings, it was also for how much fabric was used in their construction. Sadly, I never won an election in junior high. Lynn, however, won every election in which she ran. Everything she touched seemed to turn to gold. Frances continued to stoke my competitive fire, using Lynn as a symbol of success. By now, Lynn was only in competition with herself, and yet, her straight-A report cards fell short of her mother's expectations.

The one ritualistic event I never missed in junior high was the annual back-to-school slumber party held at Gail's house. A year must have been the magic length of time it took for her parents to forget the previous slumber party and be willing to host us again. It's safe to assume that no fewer than twenty girls were in attendance for a night of revelry before the fall term began.

As dawn broke, it was our tradition to leave Gail's house in our babydoll pajamas for the three-block walk to the high school campus. After singing the Blue Jay fight song and yelling a few cheers, as newly freshmen, we ambled en masse up Stockton Avenue. I doubt if anyone would admit if they could remember who first had the bright idea to drop in at classmate Tom Criswell's house.

In those days, it was not uncommon for folks to leave their homes unlocked overnight, though that was totally untrue at my house, which was secured with three locks. It took no encouragement for our mighty band to troupe right in when the Criswell's door pushed open. Parading through the downstairs, looking for Tom and his brother, Jerry, we jammed into the master bedroom to the astonishment of his abruptly awakened parents. About that time, we collectively realized we had crossed a line. We were gone in a flash, foregoing a trip upstairs to the boy's bedrooms. Good sports, the Criswells never blew the whistle on our lack of sound judgment.

Love Love

ODAY, I RARELY WEAR ANY shoe with anything but a flat heel. Why? I was told early and often that I didn't know how to walk in high heels. Maybe it was because I was never grounded. Walking around with my heels in the air kept me off balance more than I already was. I was in my late twenties when I gave in to comfort and quit trying to wear fashionable shoes. The toes on my feet did not come to a point in the middle, as was the style in dress shoes. High heels were a health hazard and only accentuated my wobbliness. Armin, one of my therapists years later, and I looked through old photos and discovered that, from a young age, when I was standing, my weight was on my heels. I used the balls of my feet and toes primarily for balance. This explained my lack of success and fear of playing net in tennis.

Tennis was a significant part of my childhood. It began in junior high. Lynn was the first to pick up a racket. Soon after, Barbara and I showed up at the college courts with borrowed rackets and a couple of used (dead) balls, curious to find out what was so great about Lynn's new interest. I have no memory that Barbara and I ever returned a ball over the net that day, though I do clearly remember walking all over those courts to retrieve the balls we couldn't hit and wondering what was so fun about tennis. Barbara soon realized the frustration and heat were not for her. But, like a moth drawn to flame, I once again locked myself in a one-down competitive dance with Lynn.

After my sufficient begging, Mother allowed me to select and charge my first racket from the nearby Thompson's Bookstore and Supply. It was a three-dollar black Spalding with silver lettering and translucent plastic strings. There was little tension in the strings. No matter how hard I swung, the ball never went far.

Physically, there was nothing about me that would suggest I was an athlete. At twelve, I was medium in height. I was slightly on the skinny side and years away from puberty. I had unusually small hands and wrists and no upper body strength. Though the proper grip and strokes were introduced in our PE class, my wrist could not maintain correct form with the impact of the ball on my strings, so most of my shots went up. Hence, I perfected my version of the lob.

This is not a recommended shot to build a game around, but a child of the 1950s learned early to use what she's got. Initially, that high ball was all I had. While Lynn was the only seventh grader to go out for the junior high team the following spring, I continued to hit with a couple of friends on the last of the six college courts.

I soon learned the downside of a lob game. The opponent was going to try to return it by smashing it back. To survive this return strategy, I grasped the importance of anticipating the ball's direction in order to run it down. I became adept at digging out my opponent's winners and realized that, if I could do this a few times in a row, the other side would become so frustrated that their balls would soon start hitting the fence. My wins were not pretty, but I was beginning to understand that what I lacked in athletic prowess, I might be able to make up by using my head and hoping my opponents might lose theirs.

Early in the eighth grade, I found a tennis book at the library that dealt solely with strategy. I learned how to disguise a lob and where and when to hit an unexpected drop shot. I bought into the book's philosophy to focus on keeping the ball in play until the opponent made the final mistake. This defensive strategy became my life mantra, "Don't give up, no matter what." Conversely, it reinforced my tendency to react to life events rather than develop a proactive approach.

That spring, I made the junior high team in the number seven spot reserved for doubles only. I was paired with a ninth grader, Phyllis Jean Warmack, who became a lifelong friend. Phyllis was amiable and accepting of everybody. She never called me a "pusher," which I'm ashamed to admit I was. As a pusher, that is, one not versed in the classic tennis stroke and prone to defensive tactics, I kept the ball in play any way possible, no matter how unorthodox my swing. I thought of myself as a human backboard, determined to chase down and return every shot my opponent hit.

After school and on weekends, I walked to the courts and hit on the backboard and with anyone there who would tolerate my unconventional style. Back home, before dinner, I continued to hit in the carport against the house. My mother would abruptly end this activity when I eventually clanged the ball into the mailbox mounted on the side of the house. Developing consistency compensated for what I lacked in power as I learned to control the ball.

Uel Bumpers had begun to see me experience a moderate level of success with no formal instruction or training. When Janie became eager to follow my lead, he drove her to Oklahoma City, Kansas City, and St. Louis for lessons with teaching professionals. She developed a classic game.

My growing interest in tennis probably stirred ambivalent feelings in my mother. She could do little to hide her young daughter's imperfection on the court other than make me the cutest tennis outfits seen at that time. My ninth grade year we played Shawnee. I was the sacrificial lamb slated to play the number one position against Patsy, the number one ranked girl in the state and two years my junior. With teammates surrounding the courts and placing bets as to how many points I might or might not win, my opponent slaughtered me, though I won occasional and meaningless points. Throughout the match, I couldn't understand my mother's continuous trilling laughter between points as Patsy blew me off the court.

Once at home, I knew I had to address a sensitive topic with my mother.

Before I could begin, Mother asked, "Did Patsy say she liked your dress?"

"No, Mother. Patsy is only twelve," I said. "I'll bet her only focus was on beating me. I don't think it mattered to her what I wore. Which brings me to something I need to tell you. Patsy is a much better player than I will ever be, but getting beat was not as hard as hearing you laugh every time I lost a point. Please don't come to any more of my matches. It's too hard to concentrate when you laugh at my mistakes."

"Be that way," she said. "I won't set foot near a tennis court again."

She didn't, and I was glad.

Lynn and her doubles partner, Patty, played the first two positions on the team. Their games were similar and complementary with hard serves, solid strokes, and, at times, flashy net play. I usually survived enough challenge matches to hang on to the number three spot. Understandably, Lynn and I did not hit together because her game was much more complete than mine.

One day, Coach Wise announced he would have room to take a few ninth graders to McAlester for a high school match.

When I raised my hand, the coach said, "If you can beat Lynn in a challenge match (win two out of three sets), you can go on the trip."

We agreed to play the next afternoon at the college. With no pretense of pleasantries, the number one player and the pusher squared off to play. I wanted so much to be accepted at this higher level that I made every effort to return each ball back as hard as Lynn hit it to me. I was quickly behind, two games to love.

As I went back to the fence to retrieve the balls, I heard Thena McBride say, "Why are you trying to play Lynn's power game? Your only chance to win is to play your own style."

Much to Lynn's consternation, I followed Thena's advice. I began lobbing, and we split sets. After a break to refill our tennis ball cans with water, we began the final set.

As play progressed, I have a vivid memory of Lynn approaching the net, hitting a winner, turning, and walking away. In the spirit of my interminable character, I made a weak, awkward stab at her passing ball. I saw my return bounce slowly by Lynn as she was striding back to prepare for the next point. Winning that point was crucial in my taking the final set.

The next afternoon, I spilled out my good news to Coach Wise as both the boys and girls teams milled around him by the gate to the junior high asphalt courts.

Coach Wise turned to Lynn and asked in an incredulous, loud voice, "Lynn, did Jill beat you?"

Members of both teams froze. All eyes were on Lynn.

No one doubted that she would beat me. The pressure to win was great.

She paused before answering, "No!"

Life for the Ada Junior High tennis teams returned to normal as I staggered away in disbelief. I did not make that trip to McAlester, but, by the next week, I had asked for a rematch, pleading with the coach that he keep our score.

The rematch was another grueling three-setter ending in diminishing daylight. The result was the same, but the coach substantiated it this time. This culminating event was the decisive turning point in my relationship with Lynn. After a relentless ten-year competition with Lynn, with that one victory, I finally gained an iota of respect from her. We never competed against each other again. Instead, we became close friends through high school and beyond.

When I was a sophomore, there was a little ninth-grade boy who appeared even less likely to succeed on a tennis court than I did. Craig was cute but small for his age. His optimistic spirit and spindly bowed legs seemed to add a spring to his step as he hustled around the court. However, it was his constant court patter that distinguished him most. A typical practice session with him went like this:

"Okay, Jilber (his favorite nickname for me), hit me some lobs," he'd say.

I'd lob one his way.

"Way too high," he complained. "Try another. Oh, that's just right."

As he swung, he said, "My overhead has improved since last week, don't you think? Maybe that's why Coach assigned us as hitting partners."

As I hit another lob his way, his chatter never slowed, "I'm hoping to make the trip for the Seminole match."

His overhead smash went awry.

"Watch out!" he hollered. "Do you think you and Phyllis will play doubles? And when are you going to get a Jack Kramer racket like the rest of us?"

As Craig smashed the final lob by me, I strolled over to the cooler for a drink and a little quiet.

More than once, before Craig's voice changed, the coach sent me, the fluffy backboard, to hit with the team's male version of Chatty Cathy. Two years later, Craig's game was much improved, and his voice had dropped an octave as we prepared to play together in the City of Ada Mixed Doubles Tournament. We successfully reached the finals, which were to be played the day after the Ada High School Junior/ Senior Prom. Our opponents would be Susan Cason (my friend Trigg's mother) and Hugh Warren (whose wife taught at our high school.)

Taking no chances that his partner might veer off the straight and narrow, Craig asked me to the prom. Susan and Hugh happened to be two of the adult chaperones. Craig took me home early to make sure I was rested for the championship match. Susan and Hugh, however, stayed until all of the kids went home. Their fatigue worked in our favor. We clinched the city crown on Sunday afternoon.

In high school, I often played the number one position on the team, but it wasn't because I was the top player. I was a sacrifice, saving our stronger players in the next three spots to enhance our chances for overall team wins. By this time, I was playing with a warped Jack Kramer racket, perfecting my spin with a concave forehand and convex backhand. However, even wearing a red tennis dress with that racket was not enough to psych the top players in Lawton or Shawnee.

Craig physically matured in college, where he developed into an outstanding player at Oklahoma State University and became champion of the Big Eight in the number one spot. In our late twenties, Craig and I teamed up again for the inaugural mixed doubles tournament at Shadow Mountain Racquet Club in Tulsa. Through our semifinals match, Craig simply placed me near the alley, and he won each match single-handedly. We both knew this strategy would not fly for the finals. Nelda Palmer was an agile, physically fit tournament player who was paired with Bart Bradley, the reigning Big Eight number one singles champion for four years running. Craig would not be able to cover for both of us, especially because they would be gunning for me. My defensive style with three hard hitters led all bettors to take Nelda and Bart.

Craig knew I was scared, but he also knew that, like him, I would not give up. Though he no longer chatted on the court, he did talk me through the match and insisted I stand at the net. I much preferred standing behind the baseline. Late in this close match, there was one critical point where Bart and I exchanged at least four volleys each at the net before I was fortunate to angle a shot by him. We won the match. Winning that silver plate with Craig is one of my fondest tennis memories.

When I meet someone today and the subject of tennis comes up, there is often an exchange of questions where each of us attempts to size up the other's ability. My most objective response to these inquiries is that I've rarely been embarrassed on a tennis court. Strangers seem to find this idea intriguing since my nonathletic appearance belies the strength of my words.

Dog Gone

THE FIRST YEAR WE LIVED on Eighth Street, we had a nondescript, dirty white dog named Peppy. An outdoors dog long before leash laws, Peppy displayed a propensity to chase cars, which often left him caked in dust from his failed efforts on our (as yet) unpaved road. I was told that Peppy had moved to a farm after he successfully caught James Dixon's right calf as he speedily pedaled by our house. I considered his departure a nonevent.

I am confident my mother would have preferred to end the presence of any animal at our house from that point forward. However, two of her sisters, Millie and Ruth, were determined that their Oklahoma niece have a pet. They drove from Alabama with two Chihuahua Manchester puppies, Duke and Duchess, the offspring of Millie's dog, Princess. They insisted I needed a pet, so Frances picked the girl dog, Duchess. Duke was soon back on the road when my aunts drove on to Montana to delight another niece with a little black ball of fur.

Duchess was distinct in looks and personality. Just over ten inches tall, she was white with a couple of golf ball-sized black spots; black, pointy ears; and a long, black nose. She knew from the beginning that she was cute and dearly loved by me. Thankfully, she was also smart because my mother took the task of dog training quite seriously. Not only did Duchess catch on to the basics, she soon mastered the tricks of standing up on two legs, circling on two legs, and rolling over on command. She would sometimes do these tricks on her own initiative to gain attention.

Duchess was also stubborn. One unusually cold winter night, I believed she would be more comfortable going outside if she wore a cute, red sweater made for dogs. It took an extra pair of hands to get the sweater on my uncooperative dog. It was not unlike leading a horse to water. Duchess refused to take even one baby step in her newly acquired outfit. She never liked to play dress-up.

As smart as she was, living with us may have been part of her developing neurotic tendencies, which were never more apparent than at the conclusion of her only pregnancy. Frances was not happy to learn of Duchess' impending motherhood. In fact, Frances was never happy to hear of anyone's impending motherhood.

Regardless, we prepared for the additions to our family. I was ecstatic at the expectation of a litter of babies while my mother hoped for a single birth. Duchess' term and size progressed until Frances finally took her to the vet for help with the delivery.

"Where are they?" I demanded, rushing in from school.

"There aren't any," my mother replied while laying down another hand of solitaire.

"What do you mean? Is Duchess okay? Where is she?" I asked.

Through this torrent of questions, my mother placidly turned over three cards at a time and said, "Duchess is gonna be all right. She is staying at the vet another night. She just had what is called a false pregnancy. She went through all the stages, but, when it was time for the birth, there was nothing there. It's not something that happens often. Let's split a Coke."

I poured four ounces each into two Howdy Doody jelly glasses and took my glass into the living room. Mother's silent acceptance of me taking a drink out of the kitchen was her acknowledgement of my disappointment. I sought solace in an episode of "Spin and Marty."

On Sunrise Lane, Duchess' bed was in my pink bathroom. At night, when she was ready to go to bed, she would drag her pale blue towel into the den. This was her way of saying, "Would someone please cover me up and tuck me in?" She slept in a ball and wanted the towel completely over her. On winter nights when the house got quiet, she would often sneak in and wait to be invited to sleep under my covers. My mother didn't like it, but she couldn't stop it.

Duchess was protective of her personal belongings and me. If a friend hit me in friendly play, she was quick to show her teeth and growl. During the seventh grade, Norris and I accidentally discovered that Duchess became agitated when we patted her pillow too hard in the living room. From there, one of us would go in the bathroom and kick her bed. She ran back and forth in a frenzy to protect her property. This is a moment now that neither Norris nor I are proud to admit, but it happened. After Norris went home, Duchess would quickly forgive me.

The prospect of a ride in the car always brought out Duchess' enthusiastic side. She mainly rode on her pillow in the back window, which allowed her to alert us to every steel girder bridge on our way. Before bucket seats and headrests, our cars had bench seats. The tops of them provided Duchess a perfect place to sit and watch for our return. If food was not involved, I was often allowed to carry her into stores.

After Duchess was accidentally caught in a closing car door, her walk appeared out of alignment, and her health deteriorated somewhat. Frances said we wouldn't have her forever. I secretly confided to Duchess that I would keep her, no matter what. The dog who silently joined me behind the sofa when I was sick deserved the return of my loyalty.

One late winter Tuesday afternoon of my junior year, Mother picked me up from school. As we pulled into the carport, she said, "I think I'll fix eggs à la goldenrod tonight."

"Fine," I thought.

Eggs à la goldenrod was my favorite dish that my mother cooked. I believe it was a popular and inexpensive dish from World War II days. I put my books on the table by the door so I could find them the next morning when I rushed off to school. I knew I had a book report due in the morning. Reading the book had been the easy part. Preparing the written report was another story, but, as usual, I could put it off until after supper. Something felt different as I walked straight through the kitchen to the bathroom off the hall. No sooner did I walk in than I walked out.

"Where's Duchess?" I demanded. "Her bed is gone, too. I don't get it."

"Oh, I had Duchess put to sleep today," she answered. "How 'bout some hot chocolate?"

"You what?" I asked. I paced into the living room so she wouldn't see my watering eyes.

"She was getting so old. She was going to have problems," she replied.

I was incensed. Back in the kitchen, I slumped on the sofa along the wall across from the table where my mother sat with her crossword puzzle while waiting for the water to boil.

"How could you do that without telling me first?" I probed in uncharacteristic fashion while fighting back a flood of tears.

"I thought you had outgrown her and wouldn't even miss her. One marshmallow or two?" she asked.

The temptation of diversion by marshmallows didn't work. I called Jane Domjanovich to meet me for a walk around the block, which was all the privacy available for my consuming grief. Jane understood. Her dog, Eenie, was special in many ways, too. I went to bed early after a silent supper, where I blotted my tears before they fell. I was angry with my mother, and she knew to keep a low profile.

The next day in English class, Mrs. Calvert asked if I was ready to give my book report.

"No, my mother put my dog to sleep without telling me," I said. The tears began to roll.

"That's okay. I know you read the book because you usually read through class," she said.

I was allowed to grieve in English class for the rest of that week. Frances never apologized for delivering my first unanticipated loss.

In retrospect, this random act of heartlessness and insensitivity could be attributed to Frances' anticipation of problems. Her method of coping was to eliminate any difficulty she could foresee. Within the first few weeks of moving on up to our nice house on Sunrise Lane, my mother called a service repairman out to remove the garbage disposal and disconnect the dishwasher. She perceived both items as having the potential to eventually become problematic at any time. Likewise, when I finished school, she had the washer and dryer removed and sold, beginning a more than thirty-year regular sojourn to the Laundromat. Because she lumped in the potential frailties of mechanical objects with my precious pet, that hurt me. Duchess was not a machine. She was my loving companion, and my mother took her from me without so much as a word of warning.

Let's Go to OU

1964–1965

THE IDEA OF GOING TO college worried me a lot. My high school academic performance was mediocre even though I enrolled in easy classes. One bleak Saturday afternoon in January 1964, my mother and I were once again discussing my college options. With my camp connections in Texas, I had it in my head that Texas Tech in Lubbock was the only school for me.

Mother had just said for the dozenth time, "If you follow such an absurd choice as West Texas with all those tumbleweeds and constant wind, should you get out there and not like it, don't think for a minute you can pack up and we'll come get you."

During round three of this monotonous discussion, the phone rang.

"Byrne?" the voice said. "It's Norris. Let's go to OU and be roommates."

Simple as that, I wearily replied, "Okay."

Until then, going to school in Norman had not seriously crossed my mind. When I got off the phone and told mother what Norris and I had decided in the blink of an eye, she retreated to the den with a book, visibly relieved.

The social impact of a ready-made roommate was the only determining factor in my higher education. The direction of my studies was of no great interest to me until a couple of years later when I realized I would have to pick a field in order to get out.

Near the end of my senior year in high school, I knew little about college life except that I now planned to go to the University of Oklahoma as Beverly had done. Because my sister was a member of the Kappa Alpha Theta sorority, I was considered a legacy. That was the limit of my knowledge of the Greek system. (I later learned that girls from Oklahoma City and Tulsa were considerably savvier about the selection process called "rush.") In the spring, I was invited to the Theta Legacy Weekend in Norman. There was no discussion. It was understood among Frances, Beverly, and me that I would accept this opportunity to meet the Thetas prior to rush in the fall.

A smallpox vaccination was required for college admission. Because I had had a severe skin problem when I was young, the requirement for this vaccination was waived when I first enrolled at Willard Elementary. Now, twelve years later, I was faced with the daunting reality of my first vaccination. Such a long period of dread and trepidation ended with nearly the whole tennis team accompanying me to the doctor's office for support one Monday after practice.

The actual vaccination inflicted less initial pain than I had anticipated, but I still became faint. I had to lie down before we left the place. Five days later, the sore on my arm was at its zenith as I left for the overnight at the Theta house. Though it looked as if a third arm were sprouting, I chose to wear a sleeveless blouse, believing it needed air more than I needed impeccable fashion. My limited social sense was apparent even to me when I arrived in Norman in a sleeveless shirt, tennis shorts, and tennis shoes. It was difficult to tell the other legacies from the college girls. Most were attired in Bermuda shorts, shirts with Peter Pan collars, and matching Papagallo flats. I had a gnawing sense that I was appearing out of place.

Small talk soon ended. We all moved to the front lawn for a civilized game of Red Rover. As I watched legacy after legacy daintily prance across the grass and lean slightly into the clasped hands of the opposing side, it was clear to me that those city girls lacked a sporting nature. Finally I was called over. No one had to tell me where the weak links were. I reared back, pawed the ground, and sailed across the grass, eagerly determined to demonstrate my knowledge and skill of the game. I broke through between two girls who hardly knew what hit them. They crumpled to the ground while my momentum carried me well past them. As I landed on the hood of a car parked on the street, I saw Thetas helping each other up. Everyone started back into the house. So much for fun and games.

The next twenty hours did not really improve for me, though to what degree the stress was building was not apparent until breakfast the next morning. The dining room was full of Thetas and legacies having breakfast and discussing the blind dates of the previous night. After going through the buffet line for rolls and juice, my Theta hostess and I joined a table of about ten girls already seated. I only remember picking up my juice glass. The next thing I knew, to my horror, I had poured juice over my sweet roll with some of it splashing well beyond my tray. Several members jumped to their feet, ready to remedy such an awkward moment by offering to get me a fresh roll. In a futile attempt to salvage my dignity, I assured them it was not necessary because I always ate my rolls that way.

I left the Theta house with great relief and an understanding that any future rush I would receive from the Thetas would be pure courtesy. It was at least three years before I could tell this story. Both the Thetas and the Kappas (where I eventually pledged) referred to this episode at rush week icebreakers for some years after.

My freshman year was a typical year of adjustment. Academically, I appeared to go to class and look at my books more than Norris, but her grade point average doubled mine. Her social life left mine in the dust, too. But, with Norris' generosity, I didn't mind. If she had a date and I didn't, she would leave me the keys to her car.

One Saturday morning, we woke early as we always did when Norris would begin to clear her sinuses. Kleenexes were then lobbed halfheartedly toward the trash can near the head of my bed. Most missed the mark. A yawn interrupted my complaint. When the yawn was over, much to my horror, my mouth didn't shut. My mouth couldn't shut. It was stuck wide open. In that position, my speech was unintelligible, but, when Norris grasped the enormity of the situation, she offered to shut it for me.

She would have had to catch me. I instinctively knew that was not a good plan. By now, I was panicked to discover I was in no position to swallow. Handing Norris the phonebook, she astutely gathered I wanted her to call for help.

She first called her dentist, but only a member of the janitorial staff answered the phone.

She then called her doctor and told the receptionist, "I know this sounds funny, but my roommate can't shut her mouth."

She then said, "Byrne, let's get dressed and go on down. They said they would work you in."

A prolonged period of not swallowing leaves more saliva gurgling around in one's throat than you can imagine. I found the proper balance by holding my head back so drool remained in check until we arrived at the front desk.

The receptionist asked, "And what is your name?"

Norris interceded on my behalf, but the overflow of a thirty-minute accumulation of saliva finally gave way. A mass of paper towels and Kleenex were absorbing my mouth's contents as we were called back to see the doctor.

"Your jaw is out of socket," he said. "Let me wrap my thumbs for protection. Then we'll see if I can fix your problem. He put his well-wrapped thumbs on my back bottom teeth, pushed down, and pulled out. With a snap, my mouth sprung closed."

He continued, "You sure do carry a lot of tension in your jaws. It might be good to look into some counseling. Once this happens, it is likely it will happen again. Let me show you how to unstick it yourself."

It was a good thing he did because it became stuck again that day at lunch. After momentary panic, I calmed down and successfully followed his directions. As for the counseling, I didn't get it, nor did I comprehend the connection he was making. Over the next twenty years, my jaws came out of socket five or six more times, often resulting in a significant shift in my bite.

Frances was intent that I do well in college. "Don't worry," she said. "I'll help you."

But she was no help when I sat for the English Proficiency Essay Test. With paralyzing indecision, I flunked on volume alone. I averaged writing less than a hundred words an hour, the equivalent of driving down the turnpike at a snail's pace. Too soon the room was empty as I labored to measure my words.

Frances did much better in Freshman Comp. She made As on my

out-of-class themes. I made Fs on my in-class themes, so we eked out a C for both semesters.

I vaguely remember an assignment in Social Work 101. Frances was diligent as she challenged the opinions of Michael Harrington, a noted authority, as he addressed issues of social change in education in a book called *The Other America*. Frances tried to lecture me on a few main points so I would not appear so clueless.

There was one day my senior year when I attempted an overnight written assignment all by myself. In a moment of rare inspiration, I was in the flow.

"This wasn't so hard," I thought. "Was I really writing this?"

"Yes!" I answered as I punctuated the closing sentence.

With a fragile sense of confidence, I turned it in. The paper came back with a B+! I was more than satisfied.

"But wait! What's this?" I thought.

A note from the professor read, "This is an excellent paper, but obviously not your work!"

I held my code of silence, not risking Frances' dependable productivity for an isolated sliver of my own success.

Wake-up Call

H AD THE OKLAHOMA SOONERS LOST their football game to the Texas
Longhorns in October 1966, Travis Lee Foster and I would never
have gone on another date, much less married. My blind date
for the OU-Texas weekend, Travis was handsome. He was tanned with
brown hair and blue eyes. He was an avid Sooners fan with a winning
smile. A Sooners victory cinched our good time. Both juniors, we continued to date each other once back on campus.

Initially, Travis was attentive and thoughtful, often surprising me
with clever, personalized gifts. Soon after we started dating, he pledged
Delta Tau Delta Fraternity. Though he showed little interest in fraternity life, he liked the fact the Delt house was in close proximity to the
Kappa house where I lived. Travis dutifully escorted me to social func-
tions, but rarely did we double-date. I attributed his social reluctance
to shyness and left it at that. My preference would have been to go out
with another couple from time to time, but I never pushed the idea on
him.

My senior year, Travis and I returned to Dallas for the annual Soon-
ers-Longhorn rivalry and to partake in the pregame revelry that accompanied the event. The downtown streets were barricaded, and the
partisan crowds in red and orange milled shoulder to shoulder. It was
an excuse to party. The spectacle typically ended with hundreds being
arrested for drunkenness and disorderly conduct, and they missed the
game the following day. The Sooners won, as they had when our dating
began. I noticed that Travis' happiness hinged on OU's winning.

In the 1960s, there was an unspoken pressure that a sorority girl
should become engaged during her senior year. Through the fall semester of that year, this subject went unmentioned between Travis and
me. Realizing a contingency plan might be necessary should Travis not

ask me to marry him, I obtained an application to teach in a Colorado suburb where my friend, Anne, was working. I exposed my lack of mathematical knowledge regarding the concept of place value when I answered the question asking what salary I would be willing to accept. Anne said the going rate was fifty-two. So when I wrote in $52,000. (Remember that it was 1968.) She quickly informed me that I was $46,800 too high.

I corrected the application, mailed it, and then began to focus on New Year's Eve plans. At the last minute, Travis decided to stay home in San Antonio rather than return early to Norman. With a new outfit already purchased, I was open to accepting a blind date arranged by my sorority sisters. It was a cohesive partying group bound for the Skirvin Hotel ballroom. I'm sure I had a better time with my outgoing date than I would have had with Travis. The amount of alcohol I consumed contributed to my willingness to be the first to dance on the table in my navy sailor minidress with red hot pants, which were actually flannel Bermuda shorts.

The last semester of my senior year began in chaos, and several events nearly prevented my graduation. In mid-January, I began a student teaching assignment at Norman's McKinley School, where I had led girls' PE classes the two years before. I misread the schedule and thought I need not attend class during my teaching. I would later discover that I had missed seven weeks of teaching methods class.

At the end of January, I received a contract offer to teach elementary school in Colorado. The thought of my leaving Travis jolted him into action. Within two weeks he proposed. On Valentine's Day, I sported an engagement ring.

While my parents had little to say about Travis, their actions said plenty. The night Travis asked my daddy's permission to marry me, Clifford granted that permission through teary eyes. In contrast, Mother began in earnest to plan her perfect wedding. That night, we agreed I would have four attendants. She selected the dress color, fabric, and pattern. Within the month, she had completed all four bridesmaids dresses. In early June, we shopped with Beverly in Dallas and found just the right wedding dress for me. It was a simple, flowing chiffon with an empire bodice of white daisies. The bridesmaids dresses were also white and trimmed in white daisy braid. I suggested a green ribbon sash, which my mother promptly nixed.

Travis and I began making plans to marry. Over spring break, I went to San Antonio to meet his family. His father was a lieutenant colonel in the Air Force and could be described as serious and a bit intimidating. I noted right away that his mother's role was to serve. By the time I stumbled out of bed at eight o'clock in the morning, she had two pies cooling, and she was icing a layer cake. I was also aware that she seemed to snag Travis' dirty clothes before they hit the bottom of the hamper. Even in my naïveté, I hoped Travis realized that his future Mrs. Foster could never strive to hold a domestic candle to his mother.

Soon after spring break, Travis and I arranged for our parents to meet at the Kappa house before all going out for dinner. Always using a critical screen when viewing my mother in public, I felt the entire event went well enough. I was quite surprised to find out later that Travis' dad had taken a strong dislike to my mother. As I think back, the colonel was probably unimpressed with a nonmilitary couple where the wife spoke up and her husband was the reticent conversant. The result of this get-acquainted effort was the news that the Fosters would make no plans to attend our wedding. The Bumpers offered to sit on Travis' side of the sanctuary.

It is fair to say that Travis may have found it hard to take as he saw me acquiesce to my mother on all wedding plans, such as the number of attendants, time of the wedding, and location of the reception. He took issue with her over several details that I didn't consider important enough to challenge. In retrospect, I recognize they were locked in a power game for control and I was their reluctant, reticent pawn.

Earlier, I described Travis as initially attentive and thoughtful. Those words later served as veils for jealous and controlling. Unless I was working, there were few instances when I was out of Travis' sight. We did everything together. He even escorted me to the Laundromat to assuage his fear that I might run into Norris or another former Kappa and become engaged in conversation beyond pleasantries. There were times he would not allow me to make a phone call, and he enforced a five-minute limit on all calls I received. Also, he kept a viselike grip on our finances. I was expected to itemize each expenditure, right down to the nickels I spent on gum.

After work, we sometimes went to the tennis courts. Though he had never played the sport, Travis had good eye-hand coordination and challenged me, the pusher, to a game. Disregarding the fragility of his ego, I gave my best on every point, and, unsurprisingly, I usually won most of them. His frustration at a girl beating him led him to take dead aim at me. My only protection was to crouch down by the net until he had fired all of his round, fuzzy ammunition at me. While I had no illusions that Travis would become less jealous or controlling, I was unprepared for him to become significantly worse immediately after the wedding ceremony in August.

Travis had ambition and a plan. I never got the picture. I had little confidence in my verbal skills in general. Where my new husband, an aspiring attorney, was concerned, I had zero confidence in my ability to hold my own with him regarding an opposing point of view. This should sound familiar. We did not argue. In my family, we discussed. My mother taught me to become mute in discussions on important topics.

She told me, "Somebody has to lose a discussion, and it will always be you."

Our social life was built on attending OU sporting events. However, if I waved to a Kappa, it might be a few days before Travis would cool off from my too friendly gesture. Another time after a home football game, the Bumpers stopped by our university housing apartment on their way home. Travis never came out of the bedroom to say hello. That fall was the first OU-Texas defeat we suffered together, and I was appalled how personally he took the loss. We had been invited to a party following the game, but he was in no mood to attend.

He said, "I don't care what you told Karen and those other Kappas. There is no way we are going to that afterparty. We made three critical mistakes. One, our offensive line was so porous that our quarterback didn't have any protection. Two, it will be a long time before I get over the coach sending in the punt team when we were on their side of the fifty. Three, penalties killed us. You can do what you want, but I'm not socializing with anybody."

We drove back to Norman and didn't even stop at Beverly's house to unwind. Travis' mood was no better the next day.

After hours of silence, he muttered, "It wouldn't hurt if you tried to cook something."

Fortunately, my parents were out of state that fall. They had gone for an extended weekend to the OU-Colorado game in Boulder. While there, my daddy got a call asking him to go to work in Devil's Lake, North Dakota. So after the game, they drove north with a weekend's worth of clothes. Eight weeks later, fearing winter on the Canadian border, my mother became so desperate to return south that she took her first and only trip by air.

Their prolonged absence during this period of marital adjustment helped to keep my issues uncomplicated with Travis. One day, I sank to the kitchen floor in despair. I had ruined another pot of beans by failing to add water at the right times. Once I put the lid on the pot, I refused to peek in to see how things were going.

My Joy of Cooking cookbook said, "Cook two or three hours."

It didn't say a word about lifting the lid or what to look for if I did. No matter how hard I tried, many of my domestic duties met with failure, and I had a husband who was quick to delineate each shortcoming. Neither of us found any joy in my cooking. A disquieting moment came when I realized with painful clarity that I had been living my entire life trying to please someone else who could not be pleased. My mother was my mother. There was nothing I could do about that. But was I really going to choose to spend the rest of my life doing what someone else (Travis) wanted? Down deep, I knew the answer was no. I did not know when I would do something about it, but, with conscious resolve, I knew I would know when enough was enough.

Travis and I were barely unpacked from our honeymoon when I began teaching at Cleveland Elementary School. The two veteran teachers on each side of my room provided a great amount of help. Team teaching was strongly encouraged. In fact, the wall separating my class and Candy Wagmon's was removable, so we collaborated daily. On the day of our first PTA meeting, Candy suggested we work on our rooms after school and then get a bite to eat before the evening meeting. She offered to give me a ride home because Travis had the car. Over dinner,

Candy shared that she was upset, and she talked about some of her marital problems. I just listened, but I was struck that the things that had upset her were commonplace to me. As I waited to cross the street after she let me off at the apartment, a car slowed to a stop. I saw the friendly face of the Kappa rush advisor, Julia Baker, an attorney from Oklahoma City. We spoke briefly.

As she drove away, she said, "Call me if you ever need to talk."

AWAKENING FROM A deep sleep, I flew out of bed at two o'clock in the morning on a mid-October Saturday. The wailing of a siren sent Travis and me to the window as we searched the calm night sky for signs of an approaching storm. Unlike the regular tornado siren and with no impending threat in sight, my imagination jumped to a civil defense event. I was immediately convinced that our country was under national attack. I believed it was futile to call anyone because death for all was imminent. Before Travis returned to bed, he attempted to calm my adrenaline rush by assuring me that it was much more likely that we would be attacked at a time our guard might be down, for example, Christmas Eve. I was consoled enough to climb back in bed and shut one eye.

On Christmas Eve, we were in Madill, Oklahoma, joining my parents who were visiting my dad's sister, Helen, and her husband, Norbert. We stayed close by in an independently owned, cozy motel. It looked like one the notorious bank robbers Bonnie and Clyde might have chosen. Each unit had its own carport, which was barely wide enough to house our Pontiac LeMans.

That night sirens went off in the wee hours. This time, as Travis had predicted, we were surely being alerted to a crisis of national scope on our most vulnerable holiday. Standing in bed, I pulled the chain to turn on the single bulb above. On closer inspection, we saw that the motel was next door to the volunteer fire department. Its members were hurrying to answer an early-morning alarm. On a personal psychological level, I realize I might have been hoping for a catastrophe because only the end of the world could resolve this mess I had married myself into. Only such a result would free me from needing to take responsibility for ending it.

Less than a month later, while visiting overnight with my parents in Ada, Travis abruptly left our card game in the kitchen and went to bed. Lying back-to-back in bed at my parents' house, we eventually fell asleep, but not before I realized I had arrived much sooner than I expected to the point where I knew enough was enough. I was acutely aware my mother was not easy for me to deal with, but I knew she was not doing anything to intentionally sabotage our marriage. I felt incapable of reversing the direction of our relationship on my own and determined it was critical that I take steps to end our marriage before children could enter and complicate the picture.

The next morning, I quietly told my mother of my decision while Travis was shaving. She told me to talk with Clifford. While Travis was studying in the den, I went with my daddy on his morning trip to the post office. Once in the car, I told him what was on my mind. Maybe because Daddy rarely said much or much less offered an opinion, when he did speak, his words had tremendous impact for me.

After I stopped rattling on, he finally said, "Well, I don't expect it's gonna get better."

That simple statement solidified my decision. Even then, I had a sense he knew what he was talking about. When I told him I was fearful to address the issue alone with Travis, he offered to get a referral for an attorney in Norman.

In less than a week, I had an appointment with a lawyer known for his tough, abrasive approach. I confided I would need him to deliver this news to Travis. It was arranged he would come to our apartment and not leave without me.

Travis picked me up at work, and we stopped for a Coke on the way home. About four thirty, I heard a knock on the door. Travis left me at the kitchen table as he turned to open the door. In the brief moment the attorney took to introduce himself and explain his purpose, Travis glanced back at me. The color in his face progressed to a point of purple. Petrified with fear, I remained seated while Travis begged to speak with me alone. I knew there was no way I could hold my own in a discussion with him. The attorney refused to leave and instructed me to pack a bag.

As I looked back from the parking lot, the image of Travis' lone, bewildered figure standing at the window seared my brain. The manner of this abrupt dissolution of our marriage, which had lasted less than six months, is the worst thing I have ever done to somebody. I still regret I had too few of life's tools to have enacted it with a more mutually satisfying result rather than such a roughshod blindside.

I consider my marriage to Travis to be a catalyst for the search for my missing self. As brief as it was, I have never regretted our marriage. The level of trauma I had with my mother was huge, and neither Travis nor I had any understanding of the damage I was carrying. Back then, no training in how to effectively communicate in a relationship was available. I only knew how to move on. I rented a basement apartment that belonged to the chapter advisor of my sorority. There I felt safe. Travis never knew where I moved.

The guilt I carried soon developed a ravenous appetite. My own interest in food dwindled to zero. A few months after my divorce, my weight had plummeted to eighty-seven pounds. My doctor prescribed a sedative to help me sleep. I took it in the bathroom while getting ready for bed. As I left the bathroom in my gown, I passed out. Twelve hours later, I woke, dehydrated and too weak to get out of bed. Later that day, I was admitted into the Norman hospital. Mark, Candy Wagmon's husband, had carried me in.

The admitting doctor stated I needed an IV. I had never heard of an IV. It sounded harmless, like a plant. I envisioned a soothing treatment room with green vines of ivy surrounding me. Not so. Because of my lifelong aversion to needles, my body's automatic defense to submerge all visible veins has been strengthened.

A nurse's several attempts to start the IV treatment in my left arm met with no success. A hasty puncture of my other arm seemed to work, and she strapped my arm to a board for stability before leaving me alone. In quiet agony, I remained as still as possible, willing my body to mirror my immobilized arm. For several hours, I tried to block out my constant discomfort. I rarely dared to peek to the side where the IV dripped.

Finally, Candy stopped in. She took one look at my arm, now ballooned to more than twice its normal size, and alerted the nursing staff that fluid was pouring under my skin rather than into a vein. Nearly a month later, others suspected I had a serious drug problem when they just saw the discoloration on the inside of my arms.

After five days, I learned of the conditions of my release. I must contact a family member, and I must agree to see a psychiatrist. I knew I was too vulnerable to handle my mother's confrontation, which prevented confiding in my daddy because he could not keep a secret from my mother. I was hesitant to tell Beverly. Trying to make a decision in such a confused state led me to think of Julia, the Oklahoma City lawyer, who had told me that I could call if I ever needed to talk. Not only did I believe she was the smartest woman I knew, she also knew Beverly when they were both at OU years before.

Julia called Beverly. Then Julia drove down from the city to see me that night. She invited me to spend some time at her house prior to returning to work. Beverly called, offering her support. She agreed to let me inform our parents in my own way.

The Byrnes expected me to call them roughly once a week. With Candy's help, I walked to a pay phone in the lobby to place the call. Immediately, they said I sounded awful. I told them I had had the Hong Kong flu.

My daddy said, "I'm going to the city tomorrow. I'll stop by."

I said, "Oh, don't."

But he did. The school secretary told him where I was. When he walked into my hospital room, I knew he needed the bed worse than I did. When he left, there was no doubt he would share this news with Frances.

My first official visit with the psychiatrist was in the hospital prior to my release. Later on, I saw my diagnosis on an insurance form: anorexia nervosa. No one I knew was familiar with the term in 1969. We all just figured it meant anxious and nervous. I was certainly a bit of both.

To her credit, Mother did not immediately jump on my case, but I knew she would not let me forget my ineptness.

During a phone conversation about a year later, Mother began a sentence totally out of the blue with, "And speaking of remembering—"

I had no idea what she was about to say. I shifted from sitting to lying on the bed, anticipating that what was about to come would hit me full force.

She continued, "The other day, I ran across your third-grade report card." She paused. "I tacked it on the wall."

I thought, "Where could this be going?"

Mother finished, "To remind me how smart you used to be."

After we hung up, I guzzled down the last half of a bottle of Bolla Valpolicella wine and called it a day.

Let the Therapy Begin

MY FIRST THERAPY SESSION IN April 1969, following my release from the hospital, did little to promise my recovery.

Before I was released from the hospital, Dr. Breickman told me to look for a two-story office building. He said I could park on the west side and come up the back stairs. As I approached the building, I was relieved to see a back entry. Otherwise, somebody I knew might have seen me entering the building from the front. It would have been obvious that I was going to an appointment with a shrink. The wide hallway had dark, wooden office doors on each side. The carpet muffled the sound of my walking. I passed Sooners Architectural Image, Redman Oil Production. Then I saw the door with the sign, "Robert E. Breickman, MD. Psychiatry."

That's it. I was there. Fortunately, the hall was empty. I self-consciously looked both ways before knocking lightly.

I thought, "I'm only doing this because they made me promise."

I opened the door, and there he was.

"Come on in," he said.

"Where should I sit?" I asked softly.

"Right over there," he replied, pointing to a velvet burgundy wing-back chair with navy piping.

He sat across from me in an identical chair. An end table was between us. A lamp with a dark accordion-pleated lampshade was on the table. The brightness of the lamp's light was confined to the three items on the table: the cover of a *Psychology Today* magazine, a pipe holder, and a box of Kleenex. I was embarrassed to see that magazine so prominently displayed. The walnut-stained paneling intensified the room's darkness. The heavy drapes were partially drawn. Only sheers protected us from about twelve inches of late afternoon sun. I was glad for this small window. Dr. Breickman carefully lit his pipe and then shifted back in his chair.

After a lengthy silence, I asked, "What should I say?"

"Anything you like," he simply replied.

That was no help. He was looking at me. Actually, he was staring. Those dark-rimmed glasses made him look too serious.

"Why doesn't he say something?" I thought. "If he's waiting for me to talk first, he's crazy!"

I thought that, if I just watched the shadow of the window pane move across the leg of my bellbottoms, he would get the idea that this wasn't working. The outfit I wore was my cutest, but it was not very comfortable with the wide belt buckle. I didn't know anybody who had ever gone to a psychiatrist, so I had no way of knowing what a typical session entailed. I didn't understand why he didn't tell me the rules first. My eyes flickered up. He stared at me. The smoke from his pipe hung in motionless suspension. Shifting my eyes downward, I stared at my pants leg. Had I not heard the ticking hum of the clock on Dr. Breickman's desk in the corner of the room, I would have thought that time was standing still. But the clock ticked. Each tick reminded me of the money I was paying for the visit. Nothing was happening. Two car doors slammed. Somebody started a car. Those people had somewhere to go, but there I sat. Until that day, I had never noticed how long one could hear a car after it pulled away.

Dr. Breickman uncrossed and crossed his legs. I heard the sound of cloth on cloth. Without looking up at him, I felt his eyes on me. The seconds ticked on. My mother would kill me if she knew where I was. I sighed deeply.

"Time's up," said Dr. Breickman.

We rose in unison. He politely opened the door for me.

"I'll see you Monday. Same time," he said.

"Okay. Bye," I replied.

As I drove home, I decided that I would give Dr. Breickman one more week. I had yet to see anything good in what I was led to believe would be the therapy I needed.

Digesting Mistakes

1969–1970

WITH LESS THAN TWO MONTHS of the school year left, I gave up therapy as I knew it and mustered enough strength and resolve to return to work. Still avoiding Travis, I spent several weekends in Oklahoma City with Julia Baker, her husband Jim, and their three children. Jim owned and managed a life insurance company. In early May, Julia and Jim invited me to go to Europe with their family for the summer with all expenses paid. I would assist in navigating their travel. Jim would fly to Europe with us, return home, and then fly back in three months to come to the States with us.

I was elated at the prospect and called home with the news.

My mother's clipped speech was predictable as she responded. "Why do you want to go over there? You haven't lost anything over there. Stupidest thing I've ever heard." I was undaunted by her barrage. Her lack of enthusiasm did not impede my departure plans. It was not something she ever told me, but I think, in some ways, she was eventually glad I made the trip because I later heard there was pride in her voice as she told people in Ada, "Oh, Jill is spending the summer in northern Italy."

This adventure provided distance from Travis and gave me a much-needed change of scenery. I resigned from the Norman Public Schools just in case an employment opportunity might materialize abroad. I left with $200 spending money and no necessary ties to return to Norman. The summer in Europe far exceeded my provincial expectations. We soon learned my navigational skills were excellent. I could read a map well. Without fail, I was able to get us anywhere we wanted to go.

After a week in London, we sailed to Holland for a few days while arrangements were made to secure a Volkswagen van. Six people and all of our luggage would not begin to squeeze into the French sedan leased for us in Paris. Directing Jim in the van around the Champs Élysées to pick up the Simca was my first challenge. The huge, circular expanse around the monument reminded me of a clock with all movement heading in a supposedly counterclockwise direction. We entered at the six o'clock position, inching and jerking along with no benefit of traffic lanes until we reached approximately ten o'clock. We then edged off onto the street and found the Simca. In caravan fashion, we began the three-day drive to Cernobbio, Italy, a quaint village on Lake Como in the northern Italian Alps. With the help of a Milano business friend, the Bakers had rented a villa, complete with a housekeeper and gardener, halfway up the mountain. Without a map and using only handwritten directions, I miraculously navigated us to the very door without a wrong turn or a need to confer with a native.

My room was upstairs. Quite narrow, it was just wide enough for a twin bed on one side and a wardrobe on the other. Its number one feature was the window with a view of the lake. The windowsill was deep enough where I could sit in it and watch the city lights of Como dance on the water at night. It was a perfect place with time to reflect and appreciate some reduction of my inner turmoil while managing in a different culture.

The morning of our first day, we woke with no electric power. When the housekeeper, Antonia, arrived, all five of us scurried around to illustrate our problem in pantomime, in lieu of the Italian language we did not speak. Antonia grabbed my arm. Chattering all the way, she led me outside and down the mountain to the building where she and Stephano lived. Once inside, she pointed to their fuse box. So our problem was solved when I returned to flip the breaker switch.

We spent weekends at the villa, choosing to travel during the week when there was less traffic on the road. Stephano and Antonia took excellent care of the property. Though our communication was difficult and clumsy, they did their best to take care of us. Every Friday afternoon, Antonia made arrangements for home-baked lasagna to be delivered to our kitchen. We would frequently return from a short shopping trip to see all our mattresses sunning in the windowsills. If we arrived home after Antonia left for the day, the house would be shuttered up so tight that it would appear that no one had been there for years. She once left us a message she had painstakingly translated from an Italian/American dictionary that read, "Shut Ever the Door, Please."

Our frequent shopping trips to the village involved stops at numerous specialty stores, including the fruit store, the milk store, and, of course, the chicken shop with whole dead, plucked birds displayed while sunbathing in the window. The highway through Cernobbio was only one lane through the shopping district, which required a policeman to stand at the dogleg point in the road to direct traffic flow. Julia often let me out near the milk store. Then she drove back and forth while I shopped. When I returned with the milk, which incidentally came in a plastic bag, the policeman would always point out the direction of our car.

As the only Americans living in the village, we stood out. The community seemed eager to facilitate our well-being. A storeowner gave me a handbook that was indispensable to our communication efforts. *I Wanna This Book* was filled with illustrations of everything imaginable, and it gave the word for each picture in six languages. This visual aid reduced my need to talk louder when I wasn't being understood, which seemed to be a universal tendency when people attempted foreign languages.

While at the villa, Julia and I adopted an Italian lifestyle centered on food and drink. With lots of pasta, pastry, and wine and no automatic disposal in the kitchen, Julia and I took on the odorous task of consuming the food left on all the plates and washing it down with our nightly bottle of vino. I should probably mention my weight gain.

Before we left Oklahoma City, the Bakers had strongly encouraged their close friends, Fred and Wanda Morris, to bring their three kids and join us in Europe. It was arranged that they would spend a few days with us at the villa and reconnect later in Florence. As the time of their arrival neared, Julia and I were in a mild panic. The villa was plenty large enough to hold five more people, but a shortage of beds was a problem.

One evening, when I was taking a walk up the mountain, I heard a man's voice say "cheerio" to his little Yorkshire terriers. So excited to hear English spoken, I followed him home. He lived at the top of the

mountain in a plush villa with an ornate swimming pool. An English-
man of German parents, he served in World War II. After the war, he
returned to Italy to marry Italy's equivalent to Mary Hart of that time.
Independently wealthy, he did not have to work. He and his wife were
greatly amused when I inquired about the possibility of a local rent-
a-bed service. They were less amused when I confused their Mercedes
as similar in appearance to our Simca. My brief story intrigued them,
and they invited me to return with my party for lunch and a swim at
the end of the week. The couple took us under their wing, helping us
make hotel reservations, taking us silk shopping, inviting us for dinner,
and, most of all, providing backup bed support for the Morris' visit.
The adventurous risk to seek and obtain their help greatly reinforced
my lessons of taking initiative, as I had learned at Camp Longhorn.

As the summer waned and no job possibility had presented itself,
we packed for our return to the United States. The Bakers were so
impressed with the way I had navigated our group that they thought
I would have potential as a travel agent. They offered to help me get
started and made clear how a write-off would be advantageous to them.
However, after investigation, I realized the training was a seven-year
duration, which was much too long for me to project at the age of
twenty-two.

I slept off jet lag in Ada. When I awoke, I stumbled into the kitchen
for a Coke, where my mother laid waiting.

"Sit down, Jill," she said. "There are some things I have to say.
I have told you many times that only your mother will tell it to you
straight and pull no punches. It's time for you to stop and think about
the harsh realities of life and all the mistakes you have made. It is obvious you have already failed as a young adult and brought the disgrace
of divorce upon your family. You don't even have a job, and you are
talking about the notion of traipsing off to Oklahoma City with not
even a warm plan in mind. Get smart! You just need to call off your
friends and settle down and live out your life here with us. You had
your chance out in the world and proved you don't have what it takes.
You can pitch in here, and we'll try to make the best of it."

She moved to her organ in the dining room and banged out a rous-
ing version of "Blame It On The Bossa Nova." I grabbed my pillow

and a few sheets and towels, loaded my clothes in the car, and took off for Oklahoma City and my future. My motivation was strong to avoid living out my life as a spinster in my parents' home.

The Bakers had told me that, if I decided to come to the city, I could stay with them for a short while until I found a job and a place to live. When I arrived at their door, plans had changed. The children's former nanny, Becky, had unexpectedly resigned from the Peace Corps, returned from her Philippines assignment, and reclaimed her old (my new) room. Julia called Wanda Morris, who agreed to put me up temporarily. Becky and I soon agreed to be roommates in a nearby furnished apartment. She found employment right away. I settled for a position as a relief switchboard operator at United Discovery Life Insurance Company, where Jim Baker was chairman of the board.

Frances could not fathom how her daughter with a teaching degree would demean herself by working relief at a switchboard. She was mortified when an Adan would say, "Oh, I saw Jill in the city."

When I was not answering the phone with, "We sell rainbows at United Discovery," I was in the stockroom, pulling staples out of stock certificates from newly purchased companies and inserting microfiche into plastic jackets. To maintain my interest in the mundane, I set daily goals to pull more staples. As my compulsivity increased, it became necessary for me to come back in the evening to achieve that growing daily challenge.

I was soon promoted to the mailroom, though my mother remained less than enthused with the news I was now pushing a grocery cart to deliver mail on each floor. Shortly thereafter, I was transferred to the investments department. This assignment provided some mental challenge, and my mother was somewhat appeased.

Jim Baker had numerous business interests. The completion of his latest project, a Hilton hotel, gave me the opportunity to work in the lobby liquor store, which required that I obtain a liquor license. I had an evening job where I was paid in liquor rather than money. My liquor cabinet was filled with the basics and a hodgepodge of exotic and international imports. (I still have a couple of bottles of Campari.) Aside from the ready availability of beverage, this position offered considerably more social exchange than what I found alone in the stockroom.

One night, the Oklahoma gubernatorial candidate, David Hall, came to the hotel. He was a handsome man with friendly blue eyes and silver hair. We had met a few years before when I was on the OU campus, and he was the guest speaker of some event. He had a knack of remembering names and faces. Back then, he said that, when he was in college, he had dated a girl from Ada named Beverly Byrne. When I told him she was my sister, he continued to speak fondly of their times together.

"Well, hi there, Jill Byrne. How in the world is your sister Beverly?" he asked.

We talked briefly before he left for the ballroom to give a speech for his gubernatorial campaign. I voted for him, and he did win. He served as Oklahoma's governor from 1970 to 1974.

Being a disappointment in life soon took on a life of its own. My social life was uneventful, limited to chance meetings with celebrities at work. I preferred to generally drink alone, which often led to calling the Bakers in a state of remorse around three thirty in the morning. Julia, Jim, and the Morris family all took turns encouraging me to go into therapy. Julia got the recommendation of a therapist she thought I would like better than the Freudian one I had stumbled upon in Norman.

To counter my financial concerns, Julia offered to pay for my counseling and let me pay her back on a timetable I could afford. I became convinced to give it another try.

The receptionist said, "Just have a seat, Jill. Dr. Kravitz will be with you soon."

"Ugh!" I thought. "She doesn't have to use my name."

The waiting room was full.

"What would people think?" I thought.

I decided to sit by the door for ten minutes. If he wasn't out in ten minutes, I would leave. It was too hard sitting there with all those people.

"What if they think I have problems as serious as theirs?" I thought. "I don't."

This wasn't even my idea. If I stopped to think, I felt worse than

I did before I came in. He had better hurry. I was startled as the door opened quickly.

"Jill Byrne?" asked Dr. Kravitz.

I swept by him into the hall, relieved to be out of the waiting room where all those people were forming opinions about the correctness of my being here.

"Second door on the left," he said.

Dr. Marvin Kravitz had eyes that, even through his wire-rimmed glasses, spelled kindness. Slightly taller than I was, he wore a charcoal suit, white shirt, and green and gold paisley tie. I wondered if the tie were a gift. It was really pretty.

Two blue, tweed club chairs faced a gray Naugahyde sofa. I gravitated to the chair furthest from the door, and Dr. Kravitz took the other one. He didn't waste time.

"How can I help you?" he asked.

I remained silent, but a reply raced through my mind.

"I'm not sure. In fact, I'm not even sure I need any help. My friend Julia really wanted me to make this appointment. She's the smartest and most successful woman I know, so I figured I'd better take her advice. I told her I can't afford it, but she said she will loan me the money and I can pay her back. Twenty dollars is a lot of money. Right now I'm making $250 a month, and rent takes a hundred of it. There's not much left, so I try not to spend. I can keep costs down with a handful of Ritz crackers and Valpolicella wine and call it dinner lots of nights.

Dr. Kravitz interrupted my thoughts, "How long have you been depressed?"

He caught me by surprise. I thought, "Depressed? Who me? Maybe I get a little down sometimes, but that's all."

"Maybe you could tell me about yourself," he said.

"Okay, but there isn't much to tell. I'm from Ada," I said. I paused. "I like to play tennis." I paused again.

Dr. Kravitz gave a slight smile.

I continued, "I got to spend last summer in Europe, but my mother didn't want me to go." I paused.

Dr. Kravitz nodded his head, encouraging me to continue.

"I've just turned twenty-four, and I don't like birthdays," I said. I paused longer. "Oh, I'm divorced."

A wave of guilt splashed over me. I had revealed way too much. But I thought I liked this man who seemed to be really listening.

"You know, Jill, anything you say here remains confidential. Tell me about your trip to Europe. Did you play any tennis?" he asked.

"Yes, we played regularly at the Villa D'Este on Lake Como. My first time on clay," I said.

My eyes drifted away from Dr. Kravitz's direction. I instead focused on the ornamental tree just outside the bank of windows along the east wall of his office. This east exposure provided shade in the late afternoon. I was glad the curtains were open. Looking out, there were no distractions, only landscaping. Telling Dr. Kravitz about my trip wasn't hard at all. He listened the entire time.

I thought, "He's going to be much better than Dr. Breickman."

Dr. Kravitz said, "You mentioned you were divorced. Would you be willing to tell me about that when we meet next week?"

"I guess," I said. "It's not something I like to talk about though."

"You don't have to tell me anything you don't want to. Let's see how you feel next week," he said.

"Okay, but don't expect much," I said.

At the door Dr. Kravitz said, "See you Thursday. Four thirty."

I replied, "Yeah. Bye."

Only a few cars remained in the parking lot. My blue-green Le-Mans waited alone on what was earlier a packed third row of cars. As I stepped off the curb, talker's remorse gripped me. I swung my foot at a piece of gravel and watched it bounce away. I was so upset with myself. I had broken the rule, "Don't ever tell, no matter what."

Almost in the Headlines

1971

THE NEWSPAPER HEADLINE "YOUNG WOMAN Slain in Kitchen" kept running through my head as I strived to keep my toes in contact with the floor. I wasn't exactly in the kitchen, but I could see it from here. I lived in a small apartment, and we were about two giant steps away from the kitchen.

It must have been something I did or didn't say. Ernie didn't look like his sweet, gentle self. In fact, I didn't really know this guy who was pinning me to the wall next to my bedroom door. Until now, I had never heard him cuss. I couldn't say I had ever seen anyone this angry. All I could do was try not to faint.

I thought he'd kill me if I fainted. He might kill me even if I didn't. Something was wrong with him. Maybe the signs were there. I just didn't want to see them.

Ernie and I had been dating off and on for about a year. We met soon after he returned from Vietnam. Most of all, I liked his sense of humor. He liked me more than I liked him. Every few months, I would say that I didn't want to get serious. He was working in a warehouse, and I didn't see any signs that he aspired to more. Each time he didn't call me for a month, I didn't give it much thought.

Dating again through the holidays, we party-hopped through New Year's Eve. After one o'clock in the morning, he brought me home, and he came inside. This all started when I fixed a scotch and water and delivered it to him on the sofa. I returned to the kitchen to pour myself some bourbon. I was about ten feet from the sofa when I saw his drink coming at me. I dodged before the glass shattered and the liquid sloshed all over my roommate's new stereo system.

I started for the door to the apartment, but he was too quick.

"God dammit! You're not going anywhere," He said.

His one yank ripped my Christmas present from him, the diamond chip necklace, from around my neck.

Ernie threw it across the room and said, "You treat me like shit. I give you this nice diamond. And what do you give me for Christmas? A shitty beer can light."

Ernie's eyes were dilated as he gripped my shoulders and banged me again and again into the wall.

"Have you even wondered why in the hell you don't hear from me after one of our serious talks?" he asked.

"No, I figure you have moved on, and we are over," I replied.

"Each time you blow me off, I shoot up. It takes me a goddamn month to clean up," he growled.

Ernie took me in his arms and cried harder than I thought a man could. My feet were on the ground.

"I'm so sorry, Jill. Please forgive me," he said.

Without warning, his anger returned, and another toe dance began. He threatened to rape me. Right now, it would not have been my first choice of things to do next, though it would have been preferable to him killing me. Ernie continued to yo-yo me up and down the wall. I was clueless until he confided he had been drinking and drugging since noon. Sometime after four o'clock in the morning, the sound of the morning newspaper being tossed against my door startled him.

"Maybe you should leave," I ventured.

"No way my woman is going to tell me what to do," he said.

"I expect Janet home anytime," I said. I stretched the truth because I knew she planned to return the following evening.

Ernie paused and gave the idea some thought. I held my breath.

"Okay, I'll leave, but I'll be back," He said.

As soon as I flipped the dead bolt behind him, I dived under my bed with the phone.

Fred Morris answered on the first ring in an attempt to not awaken Wanda, his wife.

"Ernie just left after scaring me to death. I think he's on drugs. I'm calling from under the bed," I said.

"Stay where you are. Let's not hang up. At dawn, you can get out of there and come over to our house," he said.

I spent New Year's Day and beyond on the Morris' blue leather sofa, waiting for the shakes to subside. On January 2, I had the first of three emergency appointments with Dr. Kravitz.

Meanwhile, Ernie sent flowers and a note of apology. Because no one was home to accept them, they were delivered to the apartment above mine. Though those residents were unknown to me, the guy left a note on my door.

It read, "I have some roses for you upstairs. Apartment # 203."

Ernie stopped by and misinterpreted the note. He went upstairs and broke into that apartment. He promptly trashed it.

When I returned five days later, I found a check in the mail from Ernie's father to cover everyone's damages. A note from his father accompanied the check. It closed with, "Ernie has found new work in Alaska."

"Thank God," I thought.

A Threat to National Security

O NE SUNDAY AFTERNOON IN 1973, I stopped by the Bumpers' house in Ada before heading back to Oklahoma City. I joined them at the kitchen table for a piece of fresh peach cobbler. I expressed my frustration that Mother seemed so preoccupied with America's imminent demise that she virtually ignored my news about applying for a fellowship for graduate school. Uel related to me that he had been contacted and questioned about Frances' potential as a national threat.

"Jill, I know it's hard when you come down here and all she can talk about is government crises, particularly right now while she's focused on Watergate," Uel said.

"Tell me about it," I complained.

Uel continued, "Some of those letters she writes to all the media moguls, members of Congress, and other heads of state must have racked up some concern. Early last summer, an investigative guy working with the CIA stopped by and asked me about Frances. I assured him that there was no need to worry about national security because of her. She's just an opinionated housewife with not much to do but write articulate letters where she gets a bit carried away. Personally, I thought it was pretty funny, and I told Cliff about it when he came home over Labor Day weekend."

We chuckled to think that the government considered Frances to be a potential security threat, but, as I reflected on some of the letters she wrote, I could see why they might put her in a "special" category. Frances believed the media were ruining our country. She felt that putting undeserving "nobodies" on TV made "somebodies" out of them. She wrote a scathing letter to the president of the Columbia Broadcasting Company in 1968 that said in part:

[D]isorder and violence is the dominant motif in the country, and you are the ill wind that blows the nobodies no good. To say that you disgust me is the understatement of my life, but the words, as yet, have not been invented to express my loathing. If anybody ever invents a rocket that will go all the way to Pluto, I would like to help him ... that is if the news policy-making bunch of the broadcasting companies could be the first passengers. This just goes to show you that a wee bit of violence can exist in the peace-loving heart of ... just a housewife.

In a letter to Vice President Spiro Agnew in May 1970, she continued on the same theme:

I am inclined to think that something got loose in the United States in 1960 and started to tear down the house. I cannot name it, though I can name parts of it. I think television has been the most disruptive, destructive, catastrophic force working on the modern scene. They have promoted division, sponsored anarchy, and downgraded the motives of the government until all the world is suspicious of us. Like the ever-present subversive sociology professors of the campuses, they have conducted a ten-year experiment to show that the country was built by the basest of men with the vilest of motives and the most ignoble purposes. Every day brings its quota of reiteration that the United States is the very worst country on the face of the earth.

When Watergate made the news, she continued her tirades. This time, she sent her missives to the president of the National Broadcasting Company:

Dear Sir, There is a rule in my household that the TV gets turned off for the day if Watergate is mentioned in the first sentence of the Today show. So many days broadcasting begins with Watergate that I have begun to think of TV, not as TV but as WG. The National Watergate Broadcasting Company! So there are not many days that I get to look at it any more ... The tactics of some of the TV newsmen are literally unbelievable. A classic of what I am talking about occurred a day or so ago when Frank McGee was interviewing somebody named Peter

Peterson. This man, I think, is an economist, and he came on the show to talk about the energy crisis and how it would affect business, industry, and government. Frank McGee sat there and badgered this man to make him admit that all the troubles of the energy crisis were caused by Watergate. This is hogwash and everybody knows, but this is probably the successful interview required by whoever is running TV … So there is no originality or fairness or consideration or kindness in a TV interview. The newsman has only to punch with the loaded questions and never give up punching until he gets the desired answer. That, sir, is the way it is done by people who call themselves reporters but, in reality, are propagandists … I am so fearful that our television companies are trying to become our unelected government. That a provincial little group of so-called newsmen and reporters can actually believe that New York, Washington, and the Kennedy's Boston is the heart of this nation is patently ridiculous. So I am writing this letter to call attention to the nation's need for eight or fifteen regional television broadcasting companies, completely detached and in competition with those already in existence … Congress is now completely transmogrified. It is so immersed in Watergate and impeachment that it hardly resembles a legislative body, and the business of the nation goes untended.

Interspersed between these letters to corporate officials, my mother still found time to address my young adult shortcomings in written form. I approached each familiar envelope with a degree of trepidation. I destroyed most soon after reading them, too embarrassed at her pinpoint accuracy in detailing my failure to live up to the world's expectations, which included hers. At the end, she would always add her disclaimer, professing she loved me anyway.

As the years rolled on, I destroyed her letters of attack, yet I knew she kept a carbon copy of most everything she wrote.

Frances used to say, "Jill, if you want all my letters, come on down and get them."

One day, years later, I would take her up on her offer.

Over My Head

A DRUNKEN NIGHT IN APRIL 1974 almost cost me the job that launched my twenty-plus year career in school psychology. My history with alcohol basically entailed drinking alone and turning in early. That night in April turned into an impromptu celebration with my roommates and six others involved in our graduate program in Durant, Oklahoma. The more fun and alcohol I had, the more glib and outgoing I became. Back at the apartment, my party did not end until I halfway completed a flip on my bed. Halfway through the flip, I came down on my head, and the subsequent popping noise was clearly heard by my roommate in the next room. Somewhat chagrined, but still feeling no pain, I called it a night.

After four days, I began to question whether hangovers could last this long. Dragging home from class, I dared a look in the mirror to see if I appeared anywhere close to as awful as I felt. I was startled to see my left shoulder was swollen to where it nearly grazed my earlobe.

The doctor confirmed I had torn the trapezius muscle from my skull. A neck collar, a traction contraption, and muscle relaxants became my staples.

Complications from the neck brace necessitated an extended need for the muscle relaxant prescription. In early August, I took my medication around six in the morning as my roommates and I set off for afternoon interviews in the psychological services department for Tulsa Public Schools. The first appointment was scheduled for three o'clock.

I was second. In the hall, the roommate who went first warned me, "Get ready. The director is something else."

My adrenaline raced and kicked in the pill I had taken more than nine hours earlier. By the time I sat down in the director's office, my speech was slurry, and I had to strain to hear and make sense of what she was saying. By any standards, my interview was brief and going nowhere.

As I reached the door to leave, the director asked, "Do you have a sister named Beverly?"

"Why yes, I do," I replied.

"My only teaching experience was years ago when I taught physical education for one year at Ada Junior High. Your sister is the only student I remember by name because she was so outstanding in every way. Check with my secretary if you would like to schedule a second appointment," she said.

With that familial assist, I clinched the job. After the first few rocky years, I rolled through the next twenty-five-plus years employed in the psychological services department for the Tulsa Public Schools.

Maggie and I were hired into our department within the same week in the fall of 1974. She was the same age as my sister, and she had just filed for divorce following a long marriage to a prominent homebuilder. An attractive, vibrant, middle-aged woman, Maggie was young in spirit and attitude with numerous dating opportunities once word was out that she was separated. Because we were the last hired, we were relegated to sharing a small office that was more suitable for one. Both of us were just happy to begin our professional careers that such close proximity was no problem. We, fortunately, soon became fast friends.

My desk was to the left of our door, which was on the north wall. Maggie faced east as she worked at her desk in the corner. I generally sat with my back to the wall and used the foot-long board that pulled out on the right side of my desk as my main workspace. This allowed me to face the door without my back to Maggie. Wedging my chair into the corner gave me a feeling of psychological security in a work environment that often exposed my vulnerability, particularly to our director, Dr. Mary Joe Keatley.

During our first year, our director often referred to a psychologist in the department who had resigned before the birth of her first daughter. She spoke in glowing terms of Catherine's exceptional professional skills. More than once, she showed her on videotape to make a point during staff meetings. Our colleagues who knew Catherine watched in rapt attention. I, for one, was not so enamored, and I soon became annoyed with how often her name came up.

When we returned for our second school year, we heard the enthusiastic rumble, "Catherine is coming back."

Soon, the department secretary popped her head in our office to tell Maggie she was moving up in seniority and would have the private office next door.

"Jill, you will get to share your office with Catherine Cooley," she told me.

Crestfallen at being lumped in an office with a person I thought to be a prima donna, I approached our director, begging for any other solution.

She was anything but sympathetic and showed me the door. It was no time before Catherine cheerily entered our small cubicle, only to be met with my pouting countenance. After my frosty introduction, we soon discovered our shared connection with sorority life at Oklahoma University, and I remembered her as an outstanding rushee. We also both had been hired by and shared a friendship with Bill Sullivan, an administrator of renown in the Norman school system. Soon, there was egg on my face as I, too, was happy to have Catherine back in our department.

It was funny how someone who was so terrified and paranoid about putting a word on paper would end up working in a field that demanded a written report on every student evaluated. Writing the report was the bane of my existence over my entire career, and I got through it with more than a little help from my friends. Over the years, this aspect of the job did become easier, though, relatively speaking, never easy.

There was a legend in our department about a well-liked, outgoing, and respected man who had tested all year and let his reports stack up. At the end of the school year, all of the psychologists left for the summer, and he was left alone to write up over one hundred forty reports. His paycheck was held up while he worked the next six weeks in a frenzy to complete them.

Vicarious learner that I am, I pledged then never to be more than thirty reports behind. After spring break, I would spend two or three

nights a week at Catherine's house for an enforced study hall in order
to be caught up by the end of May. Part of my hang-up was my effort
to make each one unique. Gradually, I learned they all needed to convey the specific results on the same basic information, that is, ability
level, strengths, weaknesses, and recommendations.

Through this exercise, Catherine and I grasped the fact I was well-
suited to write an excellent phrase. Sentence structure was marginal,
but a phrase was at least something to build on. Both she and Maggie
acknowledged my efforts. Over time, my confidence began to bud.
Another aspect of the expressive arts that eluded me was speaking to
a group of more than three. This was never more evident than during
the year I was forced to take my turn as president of our department.
Public speaking was an excruciating task for me, and my voice trilled
about two octaves above my normal speaking voice. I often watched
Catherine and Maggie speak publicly and marveled to hear their words
tumble sensibly out of their mouths, expressing complete sentences
and thoughts.

My first years in the department were some of my most difficult
ones in battling depression. I worried that I might commit suicide. I
typed the poem *Richard Cory* by Edwin Arlington Robinson on a sheet
of paper:

Whenever Richard Cory went down town,
We people on the pavement looked at him;
He was a gentleman from sole to crown,
Clean favored, and imperially slim.
And he was always quietly arrayed,
And he was always human when he talked;
But still he fluttered pulses when he said,
"Good-morning," and he glittered when he walked.
And he was rich—yes, richer than a king—
And admirably schooled in every grace:
In fine, we thought that he was everything
To make us wish that we were in his place.
So on we worked, and waited for the light,

And went without the meat, and cursed the bread;
And Richard Cory, one calm summer night,
Went home and put a bullet through his head.

I put the paper in an envelope and tucked it far back in one of my desk drawers. If I ever followed through on my suicidal thoughts, those who cleaned out my office desk would find the poem, my suicide note.

Our director was generally displeased with the number of students I tested, which were called my production numbers. There were people in our department who tested purely for numbers. They had well over one hundred students a year. I was one of those who intervened on the student's behalf, which made each case take longer. Therefore, my numbers were among the lowest. I worked hard to get over one hundred. If I made it to one hundred thirty-five, that was an exceptional year for me. Even more than my low numbers, our director resented my close friendships with Maggie and Catherine. Her rather accurate assessment was that their willingness to watch my back may have compromised their productivity as well.

Once over summer vacation, I heard the rumor that she hoped I would leave the department. I went straight to her office. She didn't deny it, but she only wanted to know the source of the rumor. In short, I said that the "who" didn't matter. I told her that, if she felt the same after the next school year, I would leave. With that challenge, I gave her the production number she wanted and proved to both of us that I was capable of playing a numbers game when necessary.

The number of test batteries administered was never as important to me as the difference I could possibly make in a struggling student's school and home life.

My greatest professional strength was in my conferences with parents. Without exception, I conveyed an openness that defused parental anger and angst with the school system.

One time, I tested Billy Joe Littlejohn, a sixth-grade boy who was suspended his first week of middle school for the entire school year for lobbing a pair of scissors across the classroom. While this certainly was undesirable behavior and merited appropriate punishment, there were

many more serious firearm breaches of security by other students who
were given less severe sentences.

This boy lived with his grandparents and his grandmother's senile
mother. During his lengthy suspension, he was home alone with his
great-grandmother while his grandparents worked. In my discussion
with Mrs. Littlejohn, we agreed her grandson needed to be back in
school by second semester. I scheduled a conference at the school to
consider his qualification for a transfer and subsequent placement in a
special education program.

"Good morning, Mrs. Littlejohn." I greeted Billy Joe's grandmother
as she entered the school office. "Let's go on in the conference room.
The counselor and principal will join us after the bell rings."

Very little conversation ensued before the door opened. The counselor and principal strode in along with the six teachers who had had
Billy Joe in their classrooms for one week … four months ago. The
eight faculty members resisted my suggestion that Billy Joe needed a
fresh start at another location. In a bullying fashion, all of the teachers
stated to his grandmother that they would never agree to Billy Joe's
placement in any school. In my long career, I had never witnessed
such a stacked deck. Mrs. Littlejohn didn't know what hit her as they
pressed her to sign the document that stated she agreed to permanent
homeschooling for Billy Joe.

Her silent, bowed figure brought tears to my eyes as I said, "We
need to end this meeting with no agreement reached yet."

Wiping my eyes, I followed Mrs. Littlejohn as she shuffled toward
the door to the bus stop.

I asked, "Could you come to my office in the morning so we can
figure out plan B?"

"I'll call you this afternoon and let you know if it's okay with my
boss," she said.

Later, Mrs. Littlejohn was on the phone to say she could come and
her boss was behind her all the way.

At the conclusion of our meeting, I apologized for losing my pro-
fessionalism and becoming emotional at the school conference.

"That's okay," she said. "Before I saw you were about to cry, I felt so
alone that I was ready to go ahead and do what Hazel Parker did."

"What did she do?" I asked with interest.

"Kill herself. But your tears made me know someone cared," she said.

"Don't worry," I assured her. "I will do everything I can to get Billy Joe back in school as soon as possible."

Within a week, he was transferred to another school, where he flourished in a class for children with emotional disturbances.

Locked Tight

1977

ON THE LAST DAY OF the school term, I barely made it home when I began to lock up. It was one of those rare years when I completed enough evaluations and written reports to make my quota plus five extra. However, it took an inordinate amount of energy. As I turned in the last handful of reports, I sensed the air leaving my balloon.

Change was often so difficult for me, even when the change appeared to be good. There were times when the demand to perform ruled me and the first minute of relief gave me permission to begin beating myself up in anticipation of allowing myself to do nothing. And that's what happened on my first evening of summer freedom. Maggie could see it coming, too, but it wasn't until about ten o'clock that night when I finally called to admit that I was in trouble.

Sometimes, during rough patches, she would say, "Come on over."

I was then able to drive the half-mile to her house, but not tonight. I had waited too long. By the time Maggie arrived, I had reached the door to unlock it. This was about the time my body locked up instead, and I remained propped against the wall next to the doorjamb when she stepped inside. With her help, I eventually inched the five feet to the sofa. It took a burst of anger for me to throw myself backward onto it. It wasn't exactly the preferred way to take a seat. What if my head banged and bounced against the wall? I didn't care.

She patiently sat down next to me and talked. I occasionally whispered back, expressing some of my fear and self-loathing. Maggie never gave up. When she hugged me and said I am going to get through this and have a much-earned, enjoyable summer, I was finally able to let a few tears loose. My body began to relax. This event of "How I Started My Summer Vacation" was nothing I wanted to write home about.

Jill's father, Charles Clifford Byrne, circa late 1920s.

Jill's mother, Frances Helen Woolley, late 1920s.

Beverly, Editor of the *Wee Willard News*, 1942.

Jill with Beverly in backyard on Mississippi
Avenue, circa 1950.

Jill with her
Tiny Tears
doll, First
grade, Willard
School.

Jill, Second
grade, Willard
School.
Growing
out bangs.
Frances did
not know it
was "picture
day."

Second grade play, *The Little Pink Egg*. Jill is the fifth from the right.

Lynn, Barbara, and Jill: Age 7. Jill is not happy being farthest from the camera.

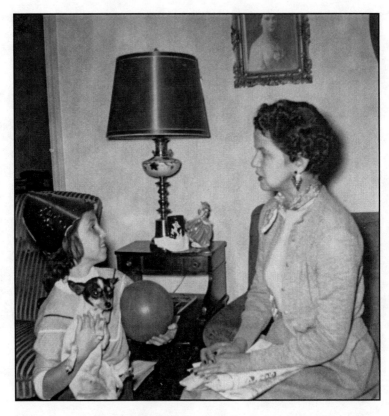

Jill, age 8, with her dog, Duchess, receiving last minute instructions from Frances before New Year's Eve.

Jill, mad about something, on the grounds of the Wyoming state capitol.

Frances resting in Cheyenne, Wyoming on vacation, 1954.

Duchess, a Chihuahua
Manchester.

Tennis team, Ada Junior High School. Jill is in the back row, fourth from the right.

Norris, Jill, and Phyllis at sorority initiation at the University of
Oklahoma. 1965.

Jill, Travis, Clifford, and Frances. How often do you see a wedding picture where the bride and her mother are not in the middle?

Playing tennis as a young adult, Jill's weight is still on her heels as she serves the ball.

Beverly and Jill with Frances and Clifford on their 50th wedding anniversary.

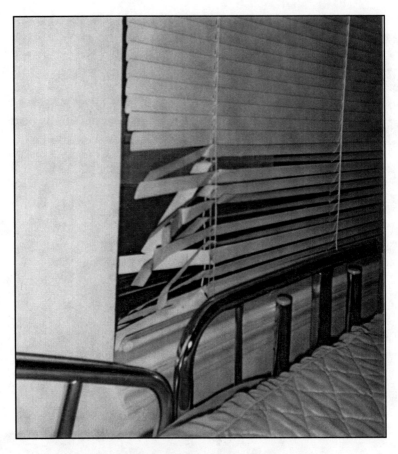

Frances' view from her bed in the nursing home.
Rather than ask for help, she preferred to see the world on her terms.

Magshots – dressed-up greeting cards. Caption reads, "Let's Party." The background is a brown piece of paper the photographer nailed into the back of an upright piano.

The Magnolias

Jill, Barbara, and Lynn enjoying an Oklabelle reunion
in New York City, summer – 2001.

Will Bioenergetics Work?

I N THE FALL OF 1975, I had three spells at work where my muscles became so rigid that I couldn't move.

Following the third one, Maggie said, "Jill, I know you haven't seen a therapist (Dr. Kravitz) since you lived in Oklahoma City. You need professional help again. As much as I want to, I'm not able to help you enough. We both know you need to be hospitalized."

"Money," I whispered.

It was the main reason I was reluctant to get help. I couldn't afford it.

"Well, I at least think you should see Armin Saeger, the licensed social worker I told you about. Shall I see if you can get an appointment?" she asked.

In defeat, I nodded okay. I knew I was stuck again. I hated it when that happened. I would shut down physically when my self-hate took over. I refused myself the luxury of doing anything in my best interest. My muscles stiffened, the noise in my head blared in an attempt to block out sounds around me, and my head and eyes lowered in shame.

I heard Maggie call the Tulsa Psychiatric Center. She was told that Armin was in session. She left a message for him to return her call. When he called back, they talked briefly, and he agreed to see me after his last appointment. That was good because we both knew it would take a while for me to get on my feet.

Maggie worked patiently, limbering my legs and hands and encouraging me to move. She asked me to mimic her breathing. She was quick to sense my waves of frustration and challenged me to help her even if I don't want to help myself.

Finally, I was on my feet, braced and ready to leave the office. Going out the emergency exit in the stockroom would save me many laborious steps and public humiliation. Besides, it was a personal emergency. Maggie walked close by my side as I inched by two office clerks. Of course, I never looked up. They had the decency to go on as if nothing unusual was happening. Getting in and out of the car was equally challenging.

Once in the reception area for the Tulsa Psychiatric Center, we stopped at the front desk. Maggie told the receptionist we were there to see Armin. I focused on the flecks in the tiles under my feet. We knew better than to take a seat, choosing instead to lean against the wall by the elevator.

I whispered, "Too much money."

Grabbing my shoulders, Maggie stepped in front of me and said, "Jill, give it up right now about the money. It's possible you are going to always need therapy, and you might as well consider paying a therapist the same way you pay any utility bill."

With that, the elevator rang, the door opened, and out stepped Armin. Introductions were made. My eyes were glued to the floor, remaining downcast. I couldn't help but notice he was wearing socks and sandals. Maggie accompanied us on the elevator. She gave Armin a bit of history as they adjusted their pace to mine while I plodded down the darkened hallway. At the door of Armin's office, Maggie said she would wait downstairs. Before leaving, she squeezed my arm and said, "You can do this."

Fortunately, the institutional chairs in Armin's office had arms, and I was able to lower myself to a sitting position, even if it was on the edge of the chair. Though I never looked up, this man with a gentle voice who just happened to wear sandals in January fascinated me. I was grateful that Armin did most of the talking. I answered a few questions in a whisper. I was impressed he was willing to tell me about himself first.

"I am a Quaker from Pennsylvania. Do you know much about Quakers?" he asked.

"No," I whispered.

"We are people who are very comfortable with silence so it's okay if you don't feel like talking sometimes. We can meet together and share the silence if that's helpful to you. I'm also a bioenergetics therapist."

"A what?" I whispered.

"We study the body and learn what it is trying to tell us. In other words, we use the language of the body to heal the problems of the mind. It probably sounds far-out, but, if you'd be willing to stand up now, I could tell you a little bit about you without you having to talk."

My hands on the chair arms, I rose on stiff legs. My eyes were focused on the gray carpet below.

"Uh-huh," he said.

"Uh-huh what?" I whispered.

"Would you mind walking to the door and back? That's enough," he said.

I returned and lowered myself back to the edge of my seat.

"Let's start with two things I observed," he said. "First, you stand and walk with your knees locked. This is a defensive posture of protection, which makes me suspect that, sometime when you were young, you needed distance in a significant relationship to feel safe. Would you stand back up? Notice that, with those locked knees, all your weight is on your heels. Your toes just provide balance. The uneven distribution of weight keeps you from being grounded and makes you a pushover."

He continued, "You can sit back down. Do you mind if I look at the bottoms of your shoes?" I let him. "Sure enough, can you see how evenly you have worn down the backs of the heels?"

With my head still down, I nodded. Even though I was still unable to look up, I was fascinated with the information and explanation. I was already applying it to my lack of success and fear of playing the net in tennis.

"The second thing I notice is your shallow breathing. Put your hand on your stomach, and take a few deep breaths. See if you can breathe deep enough to make your hand move," he said.

I couldn't.

"That's okay," he said. "That's something we can work on together. Would you be willing to come back this Friday?"

"Yes," I whispered.

"Your assignment then is to practice standing and walking with a slight bend in your knees. You will probably feel like you are going to collapse. It will take a lot of concentration at first, so take it slow and easy. You can also practice breathing deeper," he said.

He continued, "And it would be helpful if you could bring me some photos of you when you were a little girl. We can look and talk about them together. Jill, I believe I can help you if you are willing to try. We will get started next time."

"Okay," I murmured.

Armin accompanied me back to the dark reception room, now empty, except for Maggie. One thing about Maggie, I knew she cared. They exchanged pleasantries as we all moved to the door.

Armin said, "Goodbye, Jill. See you Friday."

I really liked this gentle, yet direct, man. With great concentrated effort because I wanted to show him I was willing to take this chance, I raised my head enough to finally meet his compassionate eyes.

"Oh my gosh!" I thought. "He wears a long, silver ponytail!"

"See ya," I said.

Armin strode away, and Maggie returned to my side as I continued to inch to the parking lot.

While not funny at all, I recognize that, when I am this locked up, my pace is a variation of Tim Conway's walk on the "Carol Burnett Show." It takes a tremendous amount of energy to do even the simplest task, such as getting my hair out of my face. I sometimes want to scream, but the best I can do is grit my teeth and growl. I hate it when this war inside me crescendos to a stalemate.

Maggie stayed with me until I was home in bed. She brought water for me to take a little something to relax. She didn't leave until I didn't care that she was gone.

Over the next several years, Armin continued to work hard with me, but I just wasn't a fit for bioenergetics. It meant a lot that Armin was willing to see me, and I appreciated his support. However, my body remained so tense and locked when I got close to important issues that I could not benefit substantially from his methods. Eventually and agreeably, we parted ways.

It All Happened So Fast

1977

"IT ALL HAPPENED SO FAST. And there he was, my sweet baby boy, lying there on the gravel. My cardigan sweater was all I had to pillow his head while we waited for the ambulance. He never opened his eyes, but I kept my cheek next to his so he would know I was with him."

Mascara streaked down the sides of her face as she poured another vodka straight up.

"Today is the twenty-third anniversary of Bobby's funeral service, and it is something I've never allowed myself to talk about. We had to postpone the service while waiting for the military to send Bob back home. Taking all the blame, those were the longest twelve days of my life."

"Tragic accidents happen, Beverly," said Margo, her dear friend since college days, in a soft, soothing voice. "That must have been so difficult for you."

"I was too young then to see the pattern," Beverly went on. "I would have my baby today if I had not always deferred my decisions to what somebody else wanted."

"What do you mean?" Margo asked.

"When Bob went off to Korea, I wanted to go home to Ada. But no. Bob was adamant. He wanted me to stay with his parents in Columbia. That evening, I put little Bobby in his sleepers, and he was on his way to bed. But no. Mr. Taylor insisted I bring him downstairs and for us all to go out so Bobby could watch the foreman load a couple of horses in a trailer."

"Oh, Beverly, I'm so sorry we have never talked about this. It's been too much for you to keep inside all this time," Margo said.

"I have spent the entire first fifty years of my life trying to put myself aside to please others. You guessed it. I'm mad as hell, so I say to myself, 'Have another drink, Beverly.'"

Intervention

URING THE 1960s AND EARLY 1970s, while my life yo-yoed up and down, Beverly and her family lived the upwardly mobile lifestyle. Bob was so successful in his sales career that Beverly never needed to work outside their home. They moved from one ritzy neighborhood in Dallas to the next multiple times.

Beverly wrote home on the purchase of their sixth and final house saying, "Uncle Bob bought another cabin. It will be our last move, this time to a prestigious address on Beverly Drive."

Beverly was a loving mother who ran the show with three small children close in age. When her children were in grade school, Beverly volunteered for homeroom duty and a long list of other activities. She kept all on a schedule that included fun excursions to the park for picnics, field trips to Mrs. Baird's Bakery, and the zoo. Time in the car passed quickly as she led all in song.

She played the organ for their Episcopal church. She headed up the altar guild for a larger Episcopal church they joined. She served as president for more than one term of the Theta alum group in the Dallas area. For twenty years, she modeled at the Dallas Apparel Mart. I visited as frequently as possible. Bob's work required a lot of travel, so she needed help with the kids, and I loved to do so. Beverly was appreciative and complimentary of my assistance. With her, I felt special. I never heard Beverly complain or say she was tired. However, there are photos to prove she usually watched the late movie with her eyes closed.

As the kids grew older, Beverly was sought after as the luncheon hostess in several upscale tearooms. These opportunities allowed her to forge friendships with some of the most successful chefs in Dallas, who eventually shared their trade secrets with her. Beverly became an outstanding cook and natural entertainer. Her parties held before the OU-Texas football games were legendary and, at times, included close to a hundred guests from both sides of the Oklahoma and Texas border. Though Bob prospered because of her popularity among so many influential people in Dallas, he didn't like her working outside the home. He might have thought it reflected badly on his ability to provide.

Beverly invited me down to help with their last move in the summer of 1972. The professional movers focused on furniture while the two of us moved loads of boxed items by car. Freshly shaven, Bob joined us in the kitchen, wearing Bermuda shorts, a lightly starched shirt, and Weejuns without socks to announce that he really felt like going to the lake to water-ski. He was going to see if Blane, Gail, or Nancy wanted to invite a friend to go along. After their departure, I resented carrying his extensive, heavy record collection of 78s from his high school days up from the basement into my car and then restacking them in the new basement. However, I was relieved he was not there to supervise and offer his critical suggestions.

In the summer of 1978, I enrolled in summer school at Ada's college. While my parents were out of state, I stayed in their house.

Beverly called to report, "I'm coming up to see you over the Fourth of July."

"Great," I said. "We'll have fun."

On Friday evening, as I drove home from campus and turned the corner onto Sunrise Lane, Barbra Streisand's "People" blared from our open-windowed house. It couldn't have been louder if Barbra and her twenty-piece orchestra were playing in our front yard. Beverly's yellow Cadillac Seville shone in the driveway.

Our mother rarely opened the drapes. The few times she did, she may have raised a window an inch or two. Beverly, though, had opened every curtain, shade, and window to their limits, an openness never before experienced by the owners of the house. While a part of me considered it a welcome change, Beverly's atypical lack of respect alarmed me. She mixed a drink from a portable bar in the Cadillac's trunk. She had set up another fully stocked bar in the breakfast room.

Once out of the car, I walked with hesitant steps toward Beverly. She leaned against her car with her drink in hand.

"And a cheery hello to my favorite sister," she welcomed in a voice that was too good to be true.

Beverly and I buzzed cheeks and hugged. Her cocktail dripped on my upper back.

"Hi yourself," I answered. "What time did you get here?"

"Around two" she answered. "It never occurred to me that you might be closing down the campus for the weekend. I could have used your help here."

"I would have been home had I known you were coming so early. The music's rather loud. It's probably hard on those old console speakers," I said.

"Don't worry, Jill," she said. "It's not Mother's stereo. I brought my own sound system. Isn't it great?"

"It may be a bit too much. I heard it as I turned the corner. Because the Byrnes left me in charge, I don't want the neighbors to report we disturbed their peace," I said.

"Jill, don't get heavy while I'm trying to bring a party into your life," she replied.

And an ominous party it was.

Beverly, at the age of forty-seven, appeared in the midst of a major midlife crisis. She had begun a cycle of filing for divorce from Bob, drinking erratically, demonstrating manic behavior, and then being hospitalized, which would put their divorce on hold. These behaviors signaled the onset of her bipolar mental illness.

This weekend, she was home to rendezvous with a former high school classmate, Joe. On her way, when she stopped for gas at Waupaunuka, she noticed that a man in an orange Corvette had been tailing her. He continued to stay close throughout the weekend. Beverly and her old friend took several joy rides, determined to put permanent distance between her yellow Seville and the orange Vette.

Either car on its own would have been conspicuous in Ada. Together, they caused quite a stir. Beverly and Joe enjoyed the intrigue. It drove me crazy. My worst-case scenario was the possibility of a jewel thief from Dallas who had seen the flash of her multicarat jewelry in the produce department in her neighborhood grocery store and followed her, waiting for his window of opportunity. I concluded that Bob had hired someone to keep an eye on her.

That night, the spy parked in the moonlight shadows of trees down the street. Had he known that Beverly was passed out drunk on the living room carpet, he could have called off his watch.

Beverly rose at the crack of dawn as if nothing had happened the night before. She cooked a Texas-sized breakfast spread of bacon, eggs, and toast with a potpourri of jellies and jams from Neiman Marcus. She sipped a screwdriver she had made from the bottles of vodka and orange juice near the stove.

I played in a tennis tournament over the weekend. Beverly showed up with Joe several times, talking too loud and greeting longtime Adans with an enthusiasm as large as her legend. I suspect a few saw through her façade. Concentrating on my game with my pickled sister in the stands became impossible. My game went to hell, and I didn't care because I couldn't get Beverly and Joe's partying out of my mind.

Sunday night, after the ten o'clock news, I heard a car door slam and looked out to see a shadowy figure by the curb, which I suspected to be the spy. Unnerved, I called the police. By the time they pulled in the drive, the man was gone. But they had seen the orange Vette around town during the weekend. Too scared to stay alone, I called Thena. She and her husband, Mickey, came to spend the night. Mickey packed a handgun. I slept on a pallet on the floor in my room between their twin beds.

The next morning, I decided to see Mary Gurley, a friend of Beverly's. I thought she could help me figure out what to do about my sister. I spotted Mary's car at church. Father John, an Episcopal priest and longtime family friend, was there, too. I confided with the two of them about the chaotic weekend at the Byrnes. He asked if I had heard of the Johnson Institute and the form of intervention they espouse for alcoholics in need of treatment. I said I had, but I said I would not consider addressing the subject with Beverly without his help.

He said, "How about in an hour?"

I went back home to await his visit. My sister was dressed in a crinkle designer slacks outfit in jewel tones of purple, pink, turquoise, and gold. Makeup done, she wrestled with her hair, which required a type of surgery with assorted rollers and bobby pins. The process seemed convoluted, but the result always garnered the desired look. Of course, her glass of vodka laced with a bit of orange juice and a couple of lime slices was her constant companion, even in the bathroom as she pulled herself together.

Beverly went out to the carport to hang up a small hand wash. I paced around the house, nervously awaiting Father John's visit.

As I circled back through the kitchen, I heard a car door slam and Beverly say, "Why Father John, what brings you out this fine day?"

"As a matter of fact, Beverly, I would like to talk with you. Could we go inside?" he said.

"I have no communion wine to offer. Would you like a Corona?" she offered.

"No, thank you," he replied.

"Beverly, Jill stopped by my office this morning and expressed her concern for you over the events of the last few days," he started.

Beverly shifted in her chair and glared at me with a look of unaccustomed displeasure.

My voice squeaked and cracked as I attempted to recount the general uproar of her visit. In our entire lives, we had never exchanged an unpleasant word.

Father John interrupted me, "What Jill is trying to say is that, Beverly, your behavior suggests you have a drinking problem. We are willing to help you go where you can address the issue."

Beverly looked at him and me in disbelief.

She said, "Thank you very much for your generous offer, but I can assure you and my little sister here that under no circumstances am I in need of help from either of you. And, Jill, you of all people think you can help me? You're a mental cripple who can't stand without your therapy crutch. Remember when you told me you had married our mother? You couldn't take it for six months. Turns out I did the same thing, but I had the guts to stick it out for nearly thirty years. And you are damn right, I am mad as hell, and nobody is going to tell me what to do ever again. And that includes you keeping your holy opinion of my preference to drink to yourself. Father John, I think it's time for you to leave."

"No, Beverly," said Father John. "It's time for you to leave. Frances and Clifford gave Jill responsibility for their house. If you're unwilling to acknowledge your problem, you need to go home."

"Are you kicking me out of my parent's home?" Beverly asked.

"Yes, I am," he replied.

After Beverly left, I called Bob and told him what happened. I suggested our family should plan an intervention to confront Beverly about her drinking. I thought that, if the family stood together on the matter, she might be persuaded.

Bob replied, "Well, Jill, I think that's a bit harsh. Let's just see if she comes to her senses on her own."

"If that's what you want to do, I am out of the picture. Call me if you change your mind," I said.

For the rest of the year, I had no contact with my Dallas family until Bob called on December 17.

He said, "Jill, I need your help. Your sister has gone off the deep end. She had another set of divorce papers served on me and kicked me out of the house. Even though she has turned into a big-time lush, I still love her. I don't understand where all her anger comes from after all I've done to provide for her. You were right last summer about her need for treatment. Father Willis, her favorite priest at the church, has offered to lead an intervention with you and the kids plus Trina (one of Beverly's sorority friends) and a couple other friends. I can't be there because she thinks she hates me right now."

"When should I be there?" I asked.

"It's scheduled for one o'clock Saturday at the church. Fly on down here early for the pre-meeting at ten thirty. I'll reimburse you for your plane ticket."

"Thanks," I said. "I'll go back home on the last return flight out on Saturday night."

"If I don't see you this weekend, I appreciate you stepping up and wearing the badge," Bob said.

I hung up and stepped out of my own pre-holiday funk to shift over to my power crisis mode.

The group assembled for the pre-meeting. We were all on the same page. We were concerned for Beverly, whose behavior had become so grandiose that there was question whether too much booze might not be all she was dealing with. She had recently hosted a noon to midnight gala. By now, she was living in a duplex close to the SMU campus. Because the duplex could not accommodate too large a crowd, the engraved invitations indicated which two-hour block of party time that each person should attend. She included a wide range of guests, from TV personality Art Linkletter and preacher/author Dr. Norman Vincent Peale to the grocery bag boy at the Tom Thumb where she shopped. Hundreds came in shifts, though not the big names.

Father Willis began by saying he had asked Beverly to come by his office at one. At that time, he would ask her if she would like to talk with some people who had come together to ask her to consider treatment.

I interrupted and said I believed he was presenting too many questions that required more than one decision. To me, the only question she needed to answer was whether, after listening to all of us who cared about her, she would be willing to get help. He took my suggestion to heart.

We reassembled in the church parlor after lunch. Beverly arrived on time, dressed in a bright, multicolored, polished cotton warm-up suit and a babushka over her rollers. A sweet, hail-fellow, well-met smile was on her face as she entered. Then she spotted me in the crowd.

"It's so nice to see you have come to town and didn't even call me," she said with dripping sarcasm. "Do Mother and Daddy know you are down here stirring up trouble for me, Miss Goody Two-Shoes?"

"Yes, Beverly, they know I'm here," I replied.

Father Willis redirected, "Beverly, everyone here loves and cares about you. They each have something to say. Will you listen?"

"Yes, Father Willis, I will listen to everyone except my sister. She has her own problems. She should go home and stay out of my town," she replied.

Beverly listened, drawing on her reserve of politeness as her kids and friends related their concerns and asked her to go for help. At the conclusion, Beverly rejected the suggestion to leave immediately for treatment. However, she did agree to talk with a therapist if it were a woman.

"You work it out," she said. "I'm going home."

The door slammed behind her.

With input from Beverly's friends, I found a respected woman psychologist willing to make an emergency house call on Saturday afternoon the week before Christmas. Her name was Dr. Randolph. She came to the church, and we filled her in as best we could. Then Beverly's daughter Gail and I rode with Trina, and we led her to Beverly's house.

Dr. Randolph went in to meet Beverly and ask if she would allow the three of us to join. She came back quickly to say it would not be safe, especially for me, but she didn't offer why. She went back in the house while we waited outside in the car. In less than an hour, the doctor came out to say the situation inside was extremely volatile.

"Beverly has a gun, and I urge none of you should go in. Beverly has agreed to let Blane inside to help her with the Christmas tree. My recommendation is that you begin the necessary steps with the court for an involuntary commitment," she said. Leaving that advice, Dr. Randolph got in her car and drove away.

Trina let us out at Gail's apartment and offered her help if we needed it. We called Bob to walk through the legal formalities with us. He picked us up for the short drive to the courthouse in downtown Dallas. The halls were almost empty on a late Saturday afternoon, but an after-hours judge was available to hear our account of events. He issued an order for Beverly's temporary commitment and mental status exam. He told us to appear back in his court five days later for a hearing. Arrangements were made for deputies from the sheriff's office to pick up Beverly and take her to Parkland Hospital to begin commitment proceedings.

Bob took Gail to Trina's place and dropped me off at Parkland to wait for Beverly's arrival. I expected Trina and Gail to join me before she arrived, so I was shocked down to my shoelaces when I heard Beverly spewing a string of profanity in the distance. I was mortified when she appeared from around the corner. Two deputy police officers had tightly wrapped her in a Persian carpet and were carrying her on their shoulders. Only Beverly's head protruded from this elegant straightjacket. Fortunately, Beverly did not see me. As this unlikely trio paraded down the hall to the emergency department, Beverly's tirades gradually faded. I had just witnessed my fallen heroine's darkest hour.

How much is the price of perfection? Too much. What could I do for a sister who embraced her alcoholism? Nothing.

Beverly's myth of perfection shattered for good that evening. I flew home late and returned two more times that week to help finalize the necessary legal steps.

The events of the week set me a benchmark for measuring psychic pain. I had never before seen mania or the transition from ranting, active alcoholism to a full psychotic episode. I had hoped never to see it again, but Beverly began her roller coaster rides on and off lithium. On lithium, she was fine. When she took herself off the medication, her mania resumed.

After a series of Beverly's hospitalizations, the chief psychiatrist who knew her well told me, "When your sister is admitted, at her worst, she still presents better than all the other patients. By the time she is dried out, stabilized, and near being discharged, she is so pleasant and engaging that it appears her family has done a grievous disservice to her by insisting on psychiatric inpatient care."

What Will Mother Say?

1978

FOR SOMEONE WHO HATED TO fly the friendly skies, this was the third time this week that I had mustered my courage for the forty-five-minute flight to Dallas. On the trip back to Tulsa night before last, I made the entire trip doubled over with my head on my knees, clutching a couple of airplane pillows. Part of this was due to my nerves about the flight; the other part was my anguish at dealing with my sister's raw anger. We had been negotiating with her to accept treatment at a private psychiatric facility over her current status in the hellhole of the holding tank that transferred directly into the state mental institution.

Today was her commitment hearing date. My niece Gail and I were the only family members planning to attend. Mother and Daddy knew as much as they wanted to know. I thought it was too hard for them to consider that their firstborn perfect child had turned out to be human after all.

This was the hardest thing I'd ever had to do. People say death is the hardest thing, but no one died here ... unless you counted the death of an image. In this case, we were all suffering big-time as the star of our family had exploded into full-blown mental illness.

Five long days ago, three uniformed deputies delivered Beverly to the psychiatric ward of the city's largest hospital, wrapped and rolled in a carpet with nary an overnight bag. Later that same night, Gail had returned to the locked ward to exchange a lavender sweat suit and a few permitted personal items for the rocks on her mother's fingers. It was agreed that Beverly's jewelry would safely wait out the indignity of the moment in the family lockbox.

Gail's compassion continued yesterday when she selected an outfit suitable for a courtroom appearance from her mother's closet and dropped it off at the front desk of the holding tank.

Gail and I sat together on a bench in the courthouse hallway. It seemed there was no time between the ding of the elevator and when its doors opened to announce my sister and her two deputy escorts.

By appearance, she looked great in a navy Doncaster suit with a patterned silk shell in jewel tones. If we didn't know better, we might have thought that she had arrived to accept an award for meritorious service. However, her eyes told the real truth. They were hoppin' mad. She swept by us with a look that shrunk the life out of me. The guards stopped in the doorway as she proceeded straight into the reception area and behind the first desk on her left. Beverly picked up the phone and dialed. I couldn't hear what she was saying, but her mouth didn't quit moving.

Then she motioned me over. There was a sting in her voice as I heard her say, "Here she is Mother, dear. Would you please tell your other daughter how the cow ate the cabbage?"

Beverly extended the phone to me, whapped me in the face with the receiver, and walked away. My eyes watered just as much from the smarting pain as from the uncharacteristic behavior of my beloved sister. Taken aback, I gingerly cradled the phone to my ear.

"Jill, are you there?" Mother asked.

"Yes, Mother," I replied.

"I just want to make one statement of fact. If you put Beverly away in a mental institution, I'll never forgive you. Call us when you get home tonight, honey," she said.

I hung up the phone, gently patting what was to become a discoloring bruise on my cheekbone. I hurried behind the last of the group of strangers tied to my sister's case, who were still filing in the judge's conference room. I could only hope for the best in a situation even my mother could tell was not good.

An hour later, the judge signed the commitment papers for Beverly's transfer to a private treatment site nearby.

A Gift of Family

1979-1980

THOUGH I GREW UP IN the Episcopal Church, I gave only fleeting thought to the possible existence of God. When my daddy was home, he regularly attended Sunday services. In his quiet way, he expected my mother and me to join him. He might have given me a gentle reminder to start getting ready, but he never insisted. I sometimes went. I sometimes didn't. On the mornings I didn't, he said or did nothing to provoke my guilt, which was guilt-provoking in itself. Cliff only spoke his faith through his actions. As I watched him and other adult parishioners attend regularly, I tried not to think less of them for displaying their devotion to a seemingly make-believe figure.

I was baptized at the age of six when the Byrnes joined Saint Luke's parish. In the next twenty years, three priests were successively assigned to serve our congregation. Father John was in charge fifteen of those years before being appointed a bishop in Kansas. Father John was a rather large man with a voice that needed no amplification from the pulpit. While his hairstyle may have changed with the times, I remember him best with a flattop. His wife Mary would today be described as somewhat Laura Bush-esque. While articulate and well-educated in her own right, she stayed home, raising their two daughters while Father John ran the church.

Through my first marriage and difficulties with my sister, Father John provided some counsel. However, when he referenced from the Bible, I went chilly, waiting for some opportunity to leave. As a young adult, I grew to enjoy him as a social friend because we were often at the same parties when I was home. In the summer of 1979, my religious resistance was caught off guard when I stopped by to chat with him. He asked if I had plans for after the Fourth of July. When I said no, he said he would like to sponsor me for a four-day retreat called Cursillo. On the spot, I said okay, asking no questions. And he offered no explanations.

That was a big mistake. Upon arrival, I was asked to surrender my watch and pledge to remain silent when we were outside the group meetings. The latter wasn't hard because there was no one there I knew. I quickly learned that this retreat was conducted as a renewal of faith. I felt further isolated because I knew I had no faith to renew. I resisted all overtures of friendship and acceptance and soon spoke with a priest to discuss my discomfort and desire to leave. He strongly encouraged me to stay and offered to compromise with me on aspects of the program I found offensive. So I endured.

On Sunday afternoon, there was a final ceremony. In walked a tennis friend who was thirty years my senior. Essie had come especially for me, and we returned to Ada together. The phrase "the peace that passeth all understanding" was one I had dully repeated for years. Now I heard it in a different way. By the time we arrived in Ada, I realized I was experiencing that peace for the first time. Everything was different and amazingly better. We went straight to a party at the country club, and I couldn't believe everything was so easy. I generally always had to work at any social event. Not only was I in a place I had never been before, others could actually tell a difference in me as well. For the first time, I had a true sense of the meaning of peace.

I believe the Lord used the Cursillo to finally get my attention. Until then, I did not believe there was anything greater than trying hard and mustering will power. After Cursillo, I began living with the peace that passeth all understanding. I knew it was a gift. It was not that I overtly denied the existence of God. His name just never came up. He knew the only way I could realize his existence and power was through feeling it on the inside. When I called Maggie in Tulsa, she could hear the difference in my voice. The next day, she drove down to see for herself. She had seen me and stood by me through severe periods of nonfunctioning. Her reaction confirmed my new peace.

The next two weeks were the best I'd ever spent. My interactions with others had never been smoother, and being did not take work. I could finally pray, and my prayer was one of deep gratitude.

Near the end of the second week, I joined my parents where my dad was working in Illinois. Just before I left to return to Tulsa, my mother called me aside into the kitchen.

"I don't know what is the matter with you," she said. "You are talking with way too much confidence, and it is very unbecoming. If you don't knock it off, no man is ever going to want to marry you."

My spirit-filled peace was gone in an instant. Back in Tulsa, I returned to my existence of depression alleviated by hard work. But the good news was that I could finally believe in a higher power.

Later that fall, I became active in the singles program at Asbury Methodist Church. One snowy January night, someone broke into my apartment while I was attending a Bible study. The thieves stole some silver, jewelry, and everything hanging on the walls. They even took a new tube of toothpaste and makeup from a drawer, miraculously missing my old wedding ring hidden in the back. Though I had a strong case of the heebie-jeebies, I was grateful for the support of my new church friends.

Then it happened! On the last Sunday of the month, a nice-looking man with blond hair I had never seen before sat down next to me in Sunday school. His leather jacket and well-polished boots set him apart from the suits. In the few minutes we talked, I learned his name was Quint Olson and we had tennis in common. When he told me he sold trucks for a living, I involuntarily shuddered and shifted away in my chair.

A few weeks later, I met him and some mutual friends to play mixed doubles. Afterwards, he took me in his yellow Corvette to get a Coke. As we sipped, he told me that his wife had died suddenly of an aneurysm the previous July, just before I had gone to Cursillo, leaving him with his nine-year-old son and five-year-old daughter. We both teared up occasionally as he talked.

Instinctively, I always knew I would not have any children of my own. I knew I would hurt them. I also always knew the only way I could have children was to adopt them. So right away, I felt God was giving me an opportunity for a ready-made family. However, with my background in school psychology, I was leery of taking on potential problem kids in my personal life, too. I was clear with myself that, no matter how interesting I found Quint, until I met his kids, there was no point in going out with him.

Our first date was on March 1. Quint picked me up at the door before introducing me to Brad and Mandy, who had waited in the car. On our way to the skating rink, Mandy warmed up to me in less than two minutes. Her sparkling blue eyes and fair complexion mirrored her daddy as she leaned over the seat, hoping to impress me with her three strongest attributes. Mandy announced that, at only the age of five, she could already tie, braid, and snap.

On the other hand, Brad was much more reserved and made no effort to interact beyond our introduction. Worn in a bowl cut, Brad's darker hair was as straight as Mandy's was curly. With his olive skin and blue eyes, I wondered whether Brad looked as much like their mother as Mandy resembled their father. I soon learned he was displeased that we were headed to the skating rink because he was less sure-footed on wheels than his bubbly younger sister was.

We had fun, and Brad got off the rink unscathed, appearing relieved and much more relaxed. By this point, any concerns about taking on these two precious children had melted away. From there, Quint drove on over to Southwest Boulevard to show me where he worked. He explained truck sales, and I was shocked to learn the retail price of an eighteen-wheeler.

Back at my apartment, the four of us gathered around my coffee table for a roast beef dinner. The kids seemed to enjoy sitting on the floor to eat. Brad focused on the meat and potatoes because his food allergies limited his intake of vegetables. For dessert, both kids were happy to dig into my bowl of M&Ms they had initially spotted, yet resisted, on the coffee table. Some years later, I heard Mandy's bedtime prayer as she thanked God for bringing me in her life. She said she knew I was the one to be her new mother the first time she went in my apartment and saw all those M&Ms.

After dinner, Quint called a sitter, and the two of us went to a movie he had already seen, *The Jerk* starring Steve Martin. No one in the theater enjoyed it more than we did. I was amused he could deliver many of the lines in sync with Steve. From there, we went to a coffee house for a late-night hot chocolate to talk and celebrate the success of the day. Both of us freely expressed our desire to be receptive to God's plan for our lives.

The three of them picked me up the next morning for church. I joined them for lunch and an afternoon of fun and games. Exhausted by five o'clock, I confided to Quint that I needed to go home because I was not used to this much of a social life. Needing a little space on Monday evening, I invited him for dinner on Tuesday night. He accepted. That night, March 4, we decided to get married.

The next afternoon, we met at Quint's place to tell the kids. As we came in the den, Mandy dove into my arms. Brad remained in a chair across the room. I waited anxiously for his reaction as Quint gently delivered the news. Halfway prepared for Brad to be less than enthused, I was greatly surprised and relieved when Quint explained it would mean more hugs for everyone. The smile that spread across Brad's face alleviated any residual apprehension I had carried as we all came together for a group hug and a prayer. It was an integral step in relieving a bit of their pain of the last nine months.

Prior to that weekend, I had confided to my friend and co-worker, Catherine, that there was the possibility of significant potential with Quint. I hoped I could bring him by to meet them. She excitedly left to call Rod, her husband, but she quickly returned with the news he felt that we should wait until there was a relationship. The following Monday morning in the office, she called Rod to say Quint and I had actually discussed the "m" word.

He said, "She's got to wait! We haven't even met him yet!"

They had their chance.

During my spring break, Quint took off from work a few days so we could drive to Ada and Dallas for him to meet my family and significant friends. All introductions went smoothly, and I was greatly relieved that he not only got along with my mother, but also he liked her. He clicked well with Beverly; although, still embroiled in divorce proceedings, she had another psychotic episode soon after that which prevented her from attending our wedding.

Initially, Quint felt the wedding should not take place until after the first anniversary of Sally's death. Within a few weeks, with the kids' encouragement, he reconsidered, and the date of May 10 was set. Having survived my mother's orchestration of my proper wedding in 1968, I was intent on keeping our ceremony on the simple side. In a note to Daddy, I attempted to explain:

When the minister asked if you were giving me away, I said, 'He's already done that once. It would just accentuate that he's had to keep taking me back!' So Quint and I have decided to come in together. Also nobody has to wear a tux. Most of all, thanks for being so good to me. I know at times you've really had your hands full.

Catherine and Phyllis (from Ada) took charge of planning with the church wedding coordinator while I spent as much time as possible with Brad and Mandy. Brad and I successfully shopped for a light blue three-piece wedding suit, which was not a simple task for a nine-year-old boy and his new mom-to-be. Mandy was thrilled with a new dress, which was yellow to match her naturally curly hair. We did not send out invitations, choosing to rely on word of mouth and a few personal phone calls.

The next two months were a whirlwind of activity and adjustment for everyone. A Sunday afternoon outing to the Muskogee Azalea Festival with Catherine and Rod and their daughters, Emily and Melinda, was instrumental in beginning to develop a new sense of family. We all met at my apartment. Mandy had dressed herself in shorts and a long-sleeved velour top. Quint had masterfully combed the top half of her hair. On casual inspection, the hair near her neck was a matted tangle of curls that possibly had not seen a comb for many months.

After the egg hunt on Easter Sunday, I was intent on serving egg salad sandwiches for supper. When I called for the found eggs to be brought to the kitchen, Brad, Mandy, and a few neighbor kids trailed in behind Quint, who was on roller skates. Much to their delight, he improvised a juggling routine with all the eggs until each was dropped and cracked on the floor! As I left, I remember being amused by his antic. Every kid had laughingly cheered on Quint, though none had joined in. I was relieved that I could still return to my own apartment. Little did I know that Quint would always be the biggest kid in our family. Many times, Brad and Mandy acquiesced their position to him.

When he flipped peas with his spoon at the dinner table, they pleadingly looked to me to make him stop.

Up to that time, being a member of the Olson family was certainly the best piece of my life. For the most part, I was able to keep my personal problems at bay for the sake of the children. Taking on the responsibility of parenting Brad and Mandy was not a decision I made lightly. Always to the best of my ability, I worked to keep any of my issues with Mother from oozing on to either of them. And I generally believe I succeeded in this effort.

From the beginning, Quint got along well with both of my parents. It was not hard to figure with Daddy, but I got an unexpected welcome response regarding his reaction to Mother. When the four of us went down to Ada for a day trip, Mother was always effusive in expressing to him what a great job he was doing in raising the kids.

Bless him, Quint, just as effusive, would say, "The credit goes to Jill."

Mother would say "Hmm." Then she would go on.

Prior to our arrival, she would have warned Daddy not to turn on the TV. Then, shortly into our visit, she would walk in the living room to find Daddy and Quint watching the Dallas Cowboys football game. Before she could say a thing, Daddy said, "Quint wanted to watch it." Then everything was okay.

Mother never took to the grandparent role with Beverly's children. They were so close to me in age that she instructed them to call her "Mama Frances" instead of grandmother. With Brad and Mandy's arrival, however, she relished the title of Grandmother Byrne. Once to their delight, she got into the spirit by dressing up in medical garb as she performed surgery to restore Mandy's favorite doll, Margaret. Mother generously presented Brad her old Cutlass for his sixteenth birthday before she got a new one.

All went well for the first five years of our marriage. No part of me ever considered this union could end in divorce. I had already done that once. Poorly and rather abruptly, I might add.

"Couldn't Seem to Stay Married"

1986

"HERE, YOU WANT A CHAIR?" Quint asked.

He slid open the pocket door that separated our bathroom from our walk-in closet. He placed a small Windsor rocker facing the window and backed out, shutting the door behind him. It didn't take him long to learn that I retreated to the quiet and security of my closet when I was stressed. He had seen me apply this technique before.

That was so sweet and just like Quint. I'd married a man whose moods, in any five-minute period, changed one hundred and eighty degrees and then returned to its volatile starting point. While it was difficult for me to live with this human roller coaster, I suspected it was much more difficult for him to live with himself.

Over the last few months, Quint appeared unhappy with his own life and me. At times, I suspected he felt suicidal. Quint did not have a mean bone in his body but he had many impulsive ones. The worst-case scenario would have been his rash decision to do himself in, but he would not want to leave the children because they then would have lost both natural parents. I supposed he would have thrown me in for good measure before taking the final shot.

Though I was born and raised to believe most everything wrong was my fault, I had kept things in perspective and generally succeeded in not taking his simmering rage too personally. I knew I had done nothing to purposely provoke him. But, during that afternoon on the tennis court, he had pushed me too far.

We were the defending champions of the tournament. He had never accepted my defensive style, which mirrored my general approach to life. When every shot Quint made started hitting the back fence, I sensed a growing tension between us. Stoic on the alley base-line, I watched Quint serve eight straight balls into the fence, following each with a charge to the net. Losing the game at love, Quint walked over to me in the corner.

Through clinched teeth, he said, "You have totally destroyed my serve!"

As ridiculous as I found that statement to be, it ignited my quiet anger. We returned home, defeated and unspeaking. Four hours later, I was standing by our pool when Quint came out and continued a litany of my shortcomings. He believed they had cost us the match. When I pictured myself at the bottom of the pool as the most logical escape to avoid his diatribe, I knew I was in psychological distress. Back in the house, I headed straight to our closet. Not unlike hiding between the sofa and the wall when I was young, when feeling vulnerable, I usually headed for our walk-in closet, complete with a tree-shaded window. Such a relatively small space provided the security I sought to calm down and regroup.

Hours after he had brought me the chair, I walked out. Quint lay on the bed.

When I approached, he started in with "It's all your fault—"

I never heard the end of his sentence. Shocking us both, I flipped myself into the wall between the nightstand and a five-foot-tall chest of drawers. Back on my feet, I hurled myself, with the back of the neck first, into the wall to my left, grazing my thigh on the corner of the chest as gravity took over my descent.

This human felt no pain yet. Maybe she could feel the pain, but she didn't care. She just couldn't handle another moment of everything being all her fault. Right then, she felt as if she were having an out-of-body experience. Writhing herself into a corner of the bathroom, she came to a stop with her feet in the sink and her T-shirt partially cover-ing her face on the floor. She had been depersonalized. There was no more psychic pain because the self-induced physical pain had trumped it.

The next morning, I surveyed my bruised and rug-burned body and said, "I probably need to see a therapist."

"Yeah, it's okay with me, as long as it's a woman," Quint said.

The kids and I were leaving on a driving tour to the East Coast on the last day of school. The thought entered my mind that, if I didn't find a therapist before we went, I might send the kids back to Tulsa and just get a room somewhere in the Northeast.

The day before we were set to leave, right after lunch, I remembered a woman whose children I had tested at least three years earlier. At the time, I was impressed with her ability to cope in such a stressful family situation. When I asked how she managed, she said she had been to see a counselor at the Center for Christian Counseling. Now a few years later, I didn't remember her name, but, when I called the counseling center and asked them to name their counselors, I recognized her name when I heard it. Mieke Epps. I left a message. She returned my call within the hour.

"Thanks for returning my call so quickly," I said. "I need to see someone as soon as possible, and your name came highly recommended. But first, I need to know two things. Are you at least forty years old? Can you see me in the next twenty-four hours?"

"Yes to both of those," she replied.

"Okay," I said. "When?"

"Let me check," Mieke said. She put down the phone. She soon returned. "I could see you at three thirty."

"Thank you," I said. "I'll be there."

I hung up with a sense that this woman with an accent had heard my unspoken desperation.

Meeting me in the reception area, Mieke led me to her office. She was professionally dressed. In fact, she wasn't wearing any sandals. The heels that set off her outfit gave her short frame a respectable height.

As I entered her office cubicle from the north, her life-sized forest mural covering the south wall instantly comforted me. I sat on the beige loveseat on the north wall while Mieke settled in a rocker to the left side of the mural.

She waited patiently until I was ready to speak. "It would help me to know a little bit about you first," I said.

"Okay," replied Mieke. "I was born and raised in Holland. I have been in this country since 1967 when I was hired to come work in the library. I married a man whose son and daughter moved in with us when their mother died. We had a son who is now eleven (Mandy's age). We divorced about five years ago. I went back to school and got my master's degree in social work. For the last few years, I have been working here as a licensed clinical social worker."

I was encouraged by our commonality of inheriting a boy and girl. In ready-set-go fashion, I drew a deep breath before giving Mieke my best factual account of my hitting the wall and the circumstances that led up to it. Rather than looking at Mieke, I focused on the foliage behind her. However, by the end of the review, my gaze had retreated to the minutiae of the white on my knuckles of my left fist. My head hung in shame. My body was locking up to protect the secrets and defend against my betrayal.

"What are you feeling right now?" asked Mieke.

"Don't ask me that!" I thought. I racked my brain for the right words.

What came out was, "Not good."

"Can you be more specific?" asked Mieke.

"Obviously not," I thought.

My muscles contracted as I punished myself internally for not having a good answer. I hated when this part of me took over, particularly in public. The noise in my head was as loud as Mieke's voice. I termed it as "hearing a word salad."

My mother pegged me as a first-class whiner early in my formative years. As I bought in to the number one rule of "appearance is everything," I learned how unbecoming whining could be. I liked to think I had reined in those whining impulses, but it was an area in my head where I could excel. When Mieke asked me how I felt, my internal dialog took off.

"Oh, not again! I don't know!" I thought. "This is too hard! And I don't want to play! Poooooooor me!"

Try as I may, identifying a feeling was beyond my current capability. If she had named ten feelings, I knew I could probably pick two.

Mieke left the rocker and sat on my right. When she touched my arm, I was unable to continue my personal retreat. I was grateful this professional was not repulsed by my uncontrollable, self-controlling behavior.

"Jill," she said, "you showed a lot of courage by sharing this incident with me. See if you can focus on breathing and relaxing. You are safe here."

A couple of tears began to roll. Mieke extended a box of Kleenex within my reach. When I failed to take advantage of the opportunity, she grabbed two and placed them in my hand. With clenched fist, I awkwardly wiped my face. The tears were more of relief than of sadness. I knew I needed real help. This person seemed to have accepted me without judgment.

Mieke asked, "When will you be back from your trip?"

"June 16," I replied. "Could I have an appointment sometime on the next day?"

"I'll go see if I can confirm that," she said.

She left the room, giving me a chance to get myself off the sofa unobserved. Mieke returned and handed me a mustard-colored appointment card that read, "Thursday, June 17, 1:00 p.m."

That would work. I regrouped as we chatted.

Mieke noted, "I have some very good friends who play tennis at your club."

"Is it permissible for me to ask who?" I said.

"Yes, Marchon and Betty Barone," she answered.

"Marchon was Quint's best man at our wedding," I noted.

I believed this news to be another sign that talking with Mieke was a good fit for me. I left feeling better than when I came. It was a relief to know that, with the next appointment, I had a good enough reason to return to Tulsa. Running away from my problems was no longer the option I planned to choose.

Mieke and I met regularly. My body continued to lock up when I talked about important and difficult subjects.

One day, when I arrived for our appointment, Mieke met me and said, "Let's take a walk today."

She showed great initiative. It didn't matter that it was in the midday heat of July. At least I was dressed for it. I was sorry she was in hose, heels, and a linen blazer. I didn't lock up. Again, Mieke's creativity came into play with her idea for a walk. At the conclusion of a session, she assigned homework. Twice a day I was to use Mandy's crayons to illustrate my feelings on index cards. At the next meeting, we would go through them and label them together.

Sometimes my drawings were a hodgepodge of multicolored scribbles, which we termed as anxious. One had two magic marker lines I drew to divide the card into thirds. The left side was solid in light pastels, suggesting an apprehension as I began the day. The middle was various-sized stars of primary colors, indicating my feelings of determination by midday. The right side had overlapping spirals of green, purple, and blue that we labeled as feeling a loss of control. There was one card of total black that we identified as a day I felt hopelessness and despair.

Another helpful assignment was to purchase a Velcro dartboard and not keep score. Instead, I practiced the act of letting go. One weekend, while Quint was out of town for a tennis tournament, I propped the dartboard up in a wingback chair in the living room and practiced with a high degree of accuracy. When Quint returned, my tension skyrocketed to such a degree that, not only could I not hit the target I had never missed all weekend, I now couldn't even hit the chair.

Mieke and I had a plan that, if I ever needed anything when she was out of town, my backup plan was to call the Domestic Violence Intervention Services (DVIS) office. After a tennis match over Labor Day weekend, Quint raised his voice and badgered me in the parking lot. I didn't know what to do. Because Mieke wasn't in town, I called DVIS. Their counselors weren't available on Labor Day, but I was given an appointment for the next morning. At the meeting, my counselor shared information about men who were abusive. She confirmed my family was in a potentially dangerous situation and advised me to get out of the house as quickly and carefully as I could. On Wednesday, with a trembling voice, I told Quint that I thought we needed to separate.

He replied, "Nobody's gonna kick me out of my house."

I said, "You don't have to leave. I will."

He said, "Nobody's gonna take my kids away from me."

I said, "Even though I want them as well, they can stay with you. I will never fight you for them."

Then he said, "Nobody's gonna clean me out."

I said, "You're right. I won't fight you over money because I would trust you to do the right thing by me."

Quint tearfully collapsed in my arms. His relief to not be losing much dissipated any anger that might have built within him. In only a few minutes, we wrote our financial settlement on the back of a recipe card. The next day, we told the kids. They could sense an immediate reduction in their dad's volatility and the tension between us. While understandably sad, they seemed to trust our decision.

The plan was to get through the weekend. I would then pack my bag on Monday morning after Quint went to work and the kids left for school. I called the church to see if anyone knew where I might rent a room on a temporary basis. I also let Quint's first wife's family know our situation because they had been so supportive of me.

Quint and I had each scheduled Saturday morning tennis doubles matches at the club. Of the three women with whom I played, none were close friends, and none knew of my situation. Though they had no clue what was going on within me, my atypical, outspoken behavior greatly amused them. I felt somewhat out of my body. It was like I was in a twilight zone where I had no control of my actions. I was playing the match as a metaphor for my situation.

As I ran to the net to return a short ball, I shouted, "I really don't want to do this!"

When my opponents served short to my backhand, I hollered, "I'm getting tired of this! How about changing up your serve?"

They all laughed hysterically, thinking I was kidding. Nary a smile crossed my face.

After tennis, I rushed home to make cupcakes to take to the football watch party that Quint's co-workers hosted. Mandy joined me in the kitchen where we reminisced about our times together. Then the phone rang. It was Libby, the kids' grandmother. She heard I needed a place to stay, and she had a possible solution. I was interested because no one from my church had offered any leads. Libby seemed hesitant to give me the facts.

She said, "I have a friend who has a friend who lives alone in a big house over by Utica Square. She may let you stay with her for a few weeks. There's just one problem."

"Oh no," I thought. "What could be the problem?"

Libby stammered, "She's a U-u-u-u-u-nitarian."

"Libby, let that be my biggest problem," I said. "I can handle it!"

After the game ended, Quint, Brad, Mandy, and I dined with the Cooleys. On appearance, it was just a typical Saturday night get-together, but, for me, it was a poignant evening because I knew it was all about to change. I tried hard to soak in every memory I could. The last thing I wanted was for our marriage to end, but Quint's mercurial mood swings felt increasingly unsafe for us all. Because the brunt of his growing unhappiness and discontent fell directly on me, it made perfect sense to remove the fuel (me). Then the fire (his anger) would die down. Besides, the loaded gun by his side of the bed had become more than just unsettling for me.

Right before bed, Quint growled, "You are enjoying this aren't you?"

I asked, "What do you mean?"

He said, "Look at you. You don't even seem upset, and I heard you all on the tennis court this morning. You had everybody there laughing at me."

I said, "But your name never came up. There was a lot of laughter, but they were laughing at me."

In his most snarling tone, Quint said, "I should never have agreed for you to see Mieke because she has turned you against me."

That did it.

I told him, "You have it so wrong. Mieke helped me understand that your anger is about you, not me. I am simply your safest target. I did not have to manufacture any hate toward you in retaliation, and I am not crazy for trusting you in this process."

He sobbed, and we hugged. Emotionally spent, he slept through the night.

Lying beside him, I willed sleep away so I could capture our last few hours together. My memories ran like a movie, and my tears rolled steadily until near dawn. I was experiencing an abrupt end to what had started as a charmed beginning.

On Monday morning, Quint left the house about an hour earlier than usual and without any acknowledgment of my leaving. I drove

Mandy to school. She was uncharacteristically quiet. I pulled over in the parking lot and wrote out a check for her weekly meal ticket. She fumbled with the zipper on her new backpack and stuffed the check in a side pocket.

I said, "Okay, Mandy, I know this is hard. I'm so sorry you have to go through it, but I promise you that, regardless of what happens between your dad and me, nothing changes between us. Parents may become divorced from each other, but not kids from parents. I will always love you. When I get established, you can stay with me anytime you want."

We had a long hug. She opened the door, got out, and, in no time, disappeared in a sea of sixth graders.

When I pulled up at the house, Brad was in the driveway, leaning against the hood of his new, high-gloss, black Camaro Z-28. He was showing his support for me in his own quiet way. I sensed he was relieved. Much of our mutual understanding was nonverbal yet deep.

As he got in his car and gunned the motor, I sat down on the porch step and let a few tears roll until he was well out of sight. Back in the house, I threw clothes in a bag and grabbed pillows. Quint and I agreed it would be easiest on him and the kids if they couldn't tell I was gone until we were sure if this was more than a temporary separation.

On Monday afternoon, I arrived for my regularly scheduled appointment with Mieke. The perfect weather of not too hot, not too windy, and partly cloudy sharply contrasted with the storm that rumbled through my stomach.

"Go on in, Jill. I'll be with you in a minute," Mieke said.

As I entered Mieke's office, I knew I was really wound up. I was a far cry from the Jill who frequently shuffled to this office in a depressed state and responded in agonizingly halting speech. But not this day. I was in my crisis mode. I functioned quite well in a crisis. In fact, it was the time I felt most alive. I had done an extremely hard thing that day, and I didn't think I could sit still. Maybe it would help if I sat in Mieke's rocking chair. I didn't think she would mind. The regulated movement of the chair would soothe my hyperactivity and hopefully prevent my body from immobilizing. She entered the room. Without a word, she took a seat in my usual place at the east end of her sofa.

"Can you tell me what's happened in your life since we last met?" she asked.

"You wouldn't believe all that's gone on," I replied.

"Well, tell me about it," she said.

I proceeded to recount the events of the past several days while I rocked rhythmically in the chair.

When I finished, Mieke said, "That took a lot of courage, Jill. Good job."

Those few words provided much-needed encouragement for me. I took a deep breath and exhaled slowly. A new chapter of my life was about to begin. I thanked God that Mieke would be with me to help see it through.

On my way out of Mieke's office, I mentioned to her, "I had lunch today with a good old friend who I don't see often. When we get together, we usually discover parallel turmoil in our lives. Fortunate for me, my trauma usually pales by comparison. While I was in the legal throes of committing my sister during her first major psychotic break, she was visiting her ex-husband's wife in jail. He had remarried a stripper from the Pearly Gates Club, and their life together was tumultuous at best."

I continued, "Lunch with her today was no exception. I knew it would be helpful to see her because we find ways to laugh through our troubles. Sure enough, by the time we left, my problems seemed minor in comparison."

"What do you mean?" said Mieke. "Your problems aren't minor by anyone's standards."

"Well, her daughter just married a black albino with a police record," I explained.

"You know Susie!" exclaimed Mieke.

For sure, we both did.

The next day I made a special trip to Ada to tell my parents that Quint and I were separating.

The first words from my mother's mouth were, "Poor Quint." Then her lips tightened. "You never could seem to stay married."

Changing Therapists in Midair

1987

THERAPEUTICALLY, I BEGAN TO GET better, but it was by baby steps, not dramatic leaps and bounds. I had been out of touch with any of my feelings, good or bad, for so long. Finally, I was learning to identify and express some of my feelings, the negative ones at first. I began to see and feel progress.

In one of my midday appointments with Mieke, she said, "I need to let you know some news about me. In two weeks, I'll be moving to Europe."

"Oh no!" I thought. "How could she do that?"

I had been making progress, and now I had to start all over. And it was not my fault. I would have to pay more good money to give the same background again. I wondered if Mieke saw no other way out of working with me than to leave the continent.

"What in the hell am I going to do?" I thought.

Early in therapy, Mieke had suggested I join a group at the Women's Treatment Center. Elizabeth Ingram was the therapist in charge. For the first nine months, even though I rarely said anything in group, I was impressed with Elizabeth. Short in stature and full of fun, Elizabeth stood tall in my eyes. Over that time, I appreciated her sensitivity in accepting my silence. As she did for everyone in group, Elizabeth gave me an opportunity to participate, but she never put me on the spot.

I was usually the first person out the door when group ended. One night, I hung around, waiting until everyone had left. I approached Elizabeth, explained my circumstances, and then asked if she would be willing to see me on an individual basis. She said yes.

My first appointment with Elizabeth was during the first week of October. Before we started, I needed a few answers.

I began, "Because I have to start over, not of my own choice, I need to know if you plan to move or retire in the next few years."

"No," she said. "I enjoy my work and anticipate continuing in the field for some time."

"You have seen me in group for a while," I said. "Do you have any reservations about working with me?"

"No, I realize the area of establishing trust is difficult for you. But my sense is that you are making the effort necessary for change," she replied.

"If I ever need to talk for a few minutes between appointments, would you be available if I gave you my word I would not take advantage of you?" I asked. "With Mieke, it had been helpful to call when I needed a sentence. I would use it to shut down my internal dialogue."

"I think we can handle it," she said.

"I'm willing to give this a try if you are," I said.

"Okay," she said. "Let's get started."

A month later, a train hit Elizabeth's husband, Mark, as he drove near their lakeside cabin. He remained in ICU for several weeks in a hospital that was forty-five miles from Tulsa. Mark survived, and he came home. He was later moved to a nursing home when he needed more care than Elizabeth could provide. She eventually remarried, but she remained Mark's primary care person.

I fought through my initial panic of losing two therapists in such a short time: one from a drastic relocation and the other from a life-altering accident. The latter put my difficulties in perspective. Our group continued to meet twice a month as we drove to the hospital to provide a bit of support to Elizabeth.

A few weeks later, I went to the hospital by myself. I needed to tell Elizabeth that I realized it would be some time before she would be ready to work again. I would be willing to wait if she could give me any assurance that, when she was able to return, she would start with me. In late February, she was ready.

In the belief we are given what we need, I will forever be grateful for Elizabeth's courage to work a bit outside the box with me. Had her husband's accident never occurred, no option would ever have existed with her that allowed me to experience the therapeutic situation outside of the traditional therapist-patient relationship. During my years of therapy, all the vulnerability seemed to be on my side of the table. My therapists, intentionally or not, came across as saying, "I have my life together, and you don't."

I saw my new therapist when her perfect life was torn apart and when she didn't have the pieces of her life in perfect place. Then I saw, to some degree, how she dealt with it and began to painstakingly reconstruct her life as a phoenix from the ashes. I firmly believe, had Elizabeth stayed within the restraints of her professional ethics, I would not have survived. Her willingness to allow a duality in our relationship inspired me to work hard in therapy and not take advantage of her kindness. Understandably, she struggled with this issue. In my mind, she concluded that my well-being came first. Her acceptance of me as a friend did much to still my self-destructive behavior.

My body continued to lock up in sessions when anything too personal was brought up. As with Mieke, Elizabeth and I worked that out. If my body remained locked at the end of a session, she would go on, and I would lock the door on my way out. The way they both handled this aspect of my dysfunction helped me keep my embarrassment in check. Certainly, the most difficult and longest part of my therapy was done with Elizabeth.

Signs of Slipping

O N A TRIP TO ADA in 1989, I took Mother up on her offer to give me the archive of her letters that she had copied and saved. I decided it was time to take a look at what she had written years before to CEOs, politicians, government officials, and me.

She said, "I decided you didn't want them so I tore up most of them yesterday and threw them away. Trash pickup isn't until Monday, so they're still out in the carport."

"May I go look for them?" I asked.

"I suppose so, but you probably won't find them," she said.

Once I pried off the trash can's lid, I stood back in disbelief. The trash appeared categorized, not unlike separating the whites from the colors for washing. Coffee grounds were wrapped neatly in newspaper, food scraps were securely tied in plastic bags, used Kleenexes were bundled in paper towels, and so forth. All packages were ringed with rubber bands and stacked neatly in the three-foot-high metal container.

My daddy came out for a cigarette and saw me rummaging through the trash.

This man had rarely given me a directive in my forty-plus years, but, when I told him what I was doing this day, he said, "Okay. Be sure you put everything back in there exactly as you found it, or she will get upset."

That was the day I began to realize how hard my mother was trying to keep it together.

Halfway down the can, next to a folded grocery sack of empty tin food cans, I spied the remains of her prolific writing period, compressed and bound in paper towels. I noted the four rubber bands gave the unopened package a checkerboard effect as I placed it in my car. I would save further study for later. Returning to the carport, I rearranged the remaining contents back in the can under my dad's watchful eye. He was a master at doing his part to pacify his wife's eccentricities.

When I commented about her need for organized garbage, he said, "Look under the hood of her car."

I raised the hood. Voilà! The tea party was ready. If the air filter cover could be plugged, it appeared clean enough for serving a bowl of soup. Like-new, shiny parts had been labeled with magic marker in her distinctive handwriting. It was another example of her attempt to keep everything straight as she felt her brain slipping away.

Obsessive-compulsive, that's what Frances had been over the years. I thought back to an incident a few years earlier where she spoke of the nutritional benefit of a simple bowl of cold cereal for breakfast. I had every sense of her approval when I chose this option over toast and jelly. For variety, my mother believed in systematically combining three brands of cereal in one bowl. She hovered near the kitchen counter as I correctly remembered her preferred order; Corn Flakes on the bottom, followed by Cheerios, and topped off with Rice Krispies. With growing confidence I sat down at the table.

At the moment my spoon broke the milk's surface, she went off, "Agh! What are you doing, Jill? That is not the way to stir your cereal. Not clockwise. Always counterclockwise. Now do it right."

Somewhat chagrined after breakfast, I excused myself and moved into the bedroom to make my bed. This was not a lengthy task, yet, before completion, Mother popped in to inspect.

She said, "How many times do I have to tell you? Put on your shoes to make the bed! You know it is bad business to make the bed barefooted. You are gonna break a toe, and you'll get no sympathy from me."

I held my tongue, laced up my tennies, and headed out the door. Within an hour, I had inadvertently worn out my welcome.

One Body, One Mind ... The End

I CALLED HOME ON A SUNDAY in January 1991. The phone rang and rang and rang. As I was about to hang up, Daddy answered.

"Are you in bed?" I asked, knowing the phone was on the nightstand beside him.

"Yes," he said softly.

As we talked, I noticed him slurring his words. Although it was snowing, I offered to come down.

"No, I'll be better tomorrow," he assured me.

As soon as I hung up, I called my therapist and friend, Elizabeth, to tell her of my concern. When she heard my story, she recognized a crisis about to happen. When I related my phone conversation with Daddy, she was insistent that he needed medical intervention.

"If he's not seen immediately," she said, "he could die of dehydration."

The master of understatement, I was ready to believe Daddy when he whispered he would feel better in the morning. Following Elizabeth's command, I called Mary Gurley and Jim Armstrong, family friends in Ada, to ask them to visit the Byrnes and check on Daddy.

When Mary and Jim arrived at the Byrnes' house, they tapped repeatedly on the glass of the kitchen door. They could see Frances pacing the hallway, engrossed in thought and oblivious to their presence. Frances eventually noticed them, unlocked the door, and welcomed them in with her genteel Southern flair. Jim went straight to Clifford's room, where he lay in bed. He was too weak to move. He shouted for Mary to call an ambulance. She searched frantically for a phonebook amid the kitchen clutter.

When the ambulance arrived, the paramedics rushed Daddy to the hospital with Jim at his side. Diagnosed with bilateral pneumonia and dehydration, Daddy was admitted to the hospital, only six hours after he and I ended our call.

Back home, Mary sat tight with Frances, who remained pleasant, polite, and puzzled at the turmoil. Mary told me later that she believed the weight of Clifford's physical crisis had finished off what thought processes Frances had left. Mother gazed out the living room window with a look of sadness in her eyes, standing where she had often waited for Daddy's return from his lengthy out-of-state absences.

With the state roads a weather-related mess, neither Beverly nor I could drive to Ada. Mary recruited the help of another longtime friend, Pat Younger, and they settled in for the night with Frances. None of them slept much. Preparing for a late-night snack, Mary and Pat discovered checks and bills under the table placemats. No longer sure what to do with them, Mother still knew they were important and deserved a safe place.

The next day, Beverly arrived from Dallas, shocked to learn the snowy, icy roads in the northeast part of the state would postpone my arrival. I tried to make it, but the first thirty miles of the drive were so treacherous that I crawled back to Tulsa in hopes of better road conditions the next morning. Beverly panicked at the prospect of a night alone with Mother. There was an edge in her voice on the phone as she encouraged me to hurry down in the morning. She felt the Byrnes' days of independence were over.

Upon my arrival, Beverly and I met with Daddy's doctor, who confirmed my suspicions of an even greater problem. On top of the pneumonia complications, Daddy was in the end stage of metastatic squamous cell cancer, even though a thorough medical workup thirteen months prior had revealed no presence of it.

After the doctor explained his condition to him, Daddy agreed it was time to activate the power of attorney. His main concern was for Frances' care. His next concern was more immediate. When could he have a smoke? He had had enough of the hospital's no-smoking restrictions. I told him I would work on getting him out of there as soon as we could.

Tom, an Ada friend of mine who owned a local funeral home, was a friend of Clifford's from golfing and church. He began investigating around-the-clock health care that would give Daddy the peace of dying at home. Though I greatly appreciated his efforts, I thought the task too daunting in a town as small as Ada.

The morning of January 9, I awoke early at the Byrne home, but, as usual, it wasn't before Mother. Frances had been rummaging in Beverly's room, mumbling about the cold while searching for a match. Beverly awoke when she heard Mother telling me of her search. Then she couldn't get back to sleep. She was uneasy about what Frances might do with a match should she find one. Beverly got dressed and then went to visit Daddy in the hospital while I stayed with Mother.

Frances was unwilling to leave the house. She could not locate her dentures, although she recalled tucking them in a safe place. I searched for them, which was something I had never done before. I could find keys and glasses, but no teeth. Divine guidance led me to a bathroom cabinet where I found them tucked under a Kleenex in a recycled butter container. Soon, Mother and I were off to the hospital.

At the hospital, Tom reported he could not find in-home help for Clifford. Beverly waited with Mother while I made arrangements for the Byrnes to share a room at a nursing facility a few blocks away, the Jan Francis Care Center. Tom offered to send help over to move Cliff's TV and favorite chair. I knew Daddy would be accepting of the move. I knew Mother would not.

When we returned home, I explained to Mother that Daddy was going to need nursing home care. If she wanted to be with him, both she and Daddy would need to stay at Jan Francis. Her brow knitted as she considered my words. She paced back and forth first glaring at me. Then she ignored me.

"Come on, Beverly," she said, marching into the den.

A few minutes later, I gathered up some accent pillows and other familiar small items to take to the car. Mother, with Beverly in tow, met me at the door.

She said, "Hold it right there, Jill Byrne, if you know what's good for you. Don't think for a minute you're walking out of this house with things that don't belong to you. You've been nothing but trouble here, and I'm sick of you acting like you own this place. I'm telling Clifford to send you home pronto."

With a haughty toss of her head, Mother grabbed Beverly's arm and retreated back down the hall to the den.

Meanwhile, Tom's help arrived, a truck driven by a funeral home staff member dressed in a dark suit and tie, which was typical work attire to perform an atypical task. Mother screamed when she saw him carrying the television out to the truck. She was at the door when he returned for another load. In an effort to defuse the situation, I introduced them. Mother's anger and disgust melted away as soon as her eyes took in this handsome, well-groomed man. She drew on her Scarlett O'Hara persona and thanked the man profusely for helping her and Mr. Byrne through this difficult transition.

Disaster averted with Frances, I next told Daddy the plan. He didn't care where he went as long as he could have a smoke when he got there.

The man in the suit and his truck reached the nursing home before me. The man carried Cliff's chair to his room, holding it high and upside down over his head, like he was going on safari. When I arrived, I knew how to find Daddy's room. I just followed the trail of peanuts and chip crumbs that had fallen from his chair. It was arranged for Daddy to be released from the hospital the next day and transferred to Jan Francis, where Mother would join him.

As the evening progressed, the prospect of drastic change riled Frances. Having decided I was the root of all evil, she was not about to spend the night under the same roof with me. She bolted out the door. Beverly and I caught up with her at the end of the driveway. Frances accepted my offer to take her to Jan Francis a night early. All three of us got in the car for the short drive. The on-duty nurses took the cue and escorted Mother to the room while I rushed home to pack her a bag. When I returned, Beverly was sitting in the lobby with our contrite mother.

Frances said, "If it's all right with you, Jill, I'd like to wait until tomorrow when Cliff comes."

"Sure, it's okay if you want to go home," I replied, "It's late, and we are all tired."

The three of us piled back in the car and returned home. Without another word, Frances walked back in the house and went straight to bed.

The next morning, Beverly and I were up and around, but Mother stayed in bed. I surmised she was really not sleeping in. She was rather waiting for me to leave for the hospital. Beverly disagreed. She thought Mother was avoiding the inevitable. Beverly called me at Daddy's room in the hospital to tell me that Mother sprang out of bed as soon as I backed the car out the driveway. I was right for perhaps the first time in family history.

On January 10, Frances' and Clifford's sixty-first wedding anniversary passed without celebration. Daddy's days of gaiety were long gone. His body was worn out. Mother and he shared a room.

Though he was in worse condition than she was, he could be overheard reassuring his anxious spouse, "We're going to be okay, Frances. We're going to be okay."

She pushed him in his wheelchair to the common area several times a day. She sat quietly while he puffed a Camel and then dutifully wheeled him back to their room. Ten days after his wedding anniversary, my daddy died. He had held on long enough to know that Frances would be fine without him. He and she had succeeded in their resolve to remain independent as long as possible.

Soon after Daddy died, the Jan Francis staff suggested that Mother be fitted with a hearing aid. I made arrangements for her hearing to be tested, but the man who did the testing called to say he didn't know if she needed one or not.

"What do you mean?" I asked.

"During the test, I covered my mouth and asked her to repeat the words I said. Some she did not respond to, but, when I said, 'walk,' your mother said, 'ambulate.' When I said, 'chew,' she replied 'masticate.' So go figure."

I chalked it up to Mother trying to make a good impression on an attractive, young man.

We got the hearing aid anyway, mainly to satisfy the care center staff. But our money was refunded when it was obvious she had no intention of wearing any contraption.

Transferring Daddy's estate into a trust for Mother required a great deal of paperwork, much of which she needed to sign. Mother's room-mate was livid that I seemed to be torturing her. I would enter her room with my clipboard. She would cooperate by signing two or three deeds before tiring of the ordeal and encouraging me to leave. I repeated this process every thirty minutes, to the point she hated to see me come in the door.

"Oh no. Don't you come in here," Mother whined.

"Just a couple more. Then I'll leave."

On deed number thirteen (on a stack of thirty), I watched while Mother wrote "Thena McBride" instead of her own name. Thena, her best friend, had been dead for two or three years. During Thena's final days, I had visited her. Mother knew I was now visiting her as I had Thena. I took the stack of deeds back to our lawyer, Bob Bennett, and asked if signatures on the first twelve would suffice.

The Comforts of My Closet

1993

I WAS SEARCHING THROUGH MY JOURNAL in the comforts of my closet, desperate for a sign of progress in my recent past. I found the entry, "I feel crazy when I'm the only one on the curb and no one will look over and invite me to join life's parade."

I thought, "I've got to be careful, be real still, and hold myself together a little longer. What if I can't find a therapist willing to work with me?"

It was the Fourth of July. People were celebrating Independence Day, and, once again, I didn't get to join. This isolation felt familiar. Only six months ago, I waited all day for someone, anyone, to stop by or call. Nobody did. Just in case, I was determined to be ready, so I paced without sitting from ten o'clock in the morning until dark. It was a fine practice of self-control. By then, my disappointment was secondary to the physical anguish of my screaming calves. I couldn't swear that anyone said he might come over. The drugs still seemed to soften my thinking to the point that I didn't know what I was doing or why I was doing it.

When my isolation grows to an agonizing level, I feel most like giving up because I see no potential for things to be less hard.

Right now, here in the closet was the safest place for me. Some people were surprised to learn of my personal difficulties with depression. That was because they didn't see me unless I believed I could go out and act normal. Rarely did I overestimate my abilities.

I didn't know how to explain the comfort I find in the constraints of this small space. Removing the two suitcases that usually held this spot, there was just enough room for me to curl up with my pillow, Buttermilk. It's been said that two negatives make a positive, so I hoped this darkness and the darkness in my heart would find a ray of light soon.

"How long should I wait?" I thought.

I wasn't ready for Mother to die. When she did, I would lose all hope that she would become a positive, healthy force in my life. She would never be able to undo the damage I absorbed. There were points where the fear of her censure and ridicule had been all that kept me going. I know I would soon have nothing as strong as that internal angst.

"Which is better?" I thought. "Crazy or dead? Today, it's a toss-up."

I was in a personal war about money. As I continually spent on my mental health, Beverly saved her money rather than invested in therapy. We resembled the radical approaches of the two little pigs. Neither of us knew which one of us was building our house of bricks. Tonight, I felt knee-deep in straw. I had enough savings to settle my Summerhill inpatient account tomorrow.

"Maybe I will next week?" I thought.

I began my next day's journal entry with, "Yes, I lived my mantra yesterday. I was careful, real still, and held myself together well enough."

Tap Shoes in Bed

PSYCHOTIC EPISODES CAN BE DEVIOUS creatures, lurking around darkened corners and leaping out to snare their unsuspecting victims. Mine overtook me in such a fashion. Neither Elizabeth, my therapist whom I had been seeing weekly for five years, nor my friends, family, and colleagues at work saw it coming. In 1992, though my life's troubled waters continued to churn, Elizabeth was my lifeboat. With her help, I was coping with events of the previous year, including my father's decline and death and my mother's move to a nursing home. In the spring, I moved to a cute bungalow home just right for me, hoping for a fresh start. Spring turned to summer, and summer turned to fall. The year was passing.

I have never liked Novembers. The month has far too little sunlight. The first day of this one, a dreary Sunday, began on an ominous note. I awakened in the early-morning hours with an excruciating pain in my stomach.

"It's something I ate," I rationalized, but the pain only intensified as the day went along.

Later that evening, doubled over in agony, I drove to the minor emergency room at Springer Clinic, where I was diagnosed with a likely case of diverticulitis.

"Bactrim should help the pain," said Dr. Harrison as he wrote out the prescription for me. "I want to see you tomorrow so we can run some additional tests."

Bactrim was a heavy-duty antibiotic, which I had never taken. Dr. Harrison knew I was allergic to penicillin, and he assumed Bactrim would be an effective alternative.

At work on Monday morning, I began to feel strange in a variety of ways. Initially, I felt I might faint or vomit, and every nerve in my body seemed to be on high alert. Try as I might, I couldn't concentrate on conversations with my co-workers. I was with them when they started a sentence, but, by mid-sentence, my thoughts were floating off to other places.

"Why can't I focus?" I thought.

It frightened me to think I was losing control. But even those thoughts were hard for me to form. I knew I couldn't wait for my afternoon appointment, so I abruptly left work and drove the two miles to Dr. Harrison's office. He ordered a lower GI series of tests where they used a clear liquid rather than the barium that requires a night's prep. The tests confirmed diverticulitis. Dr. Harrison said I should continue taking the Bactrim. He sent me home with orders to get some rest. At home, my ability to sleep deteriorated rapidly.

At two o'clock in the morning on Wednesday, as I turned a corner in my sleep-deprived mind, the episode jumped from the shadows and grabbed me. In its grasp, I saw and felt things I had never experienced before and wanted never to experience again. Without warning or fanfare, I saw the inside of my brain. It was fascinating at the time. I felt I had been chosen to see the inner workings of the mind, and it would be my job to impart this new knowledge to the world's scientific community.

In spite of the early hour, I phoned a few friends to share my discovery. Sue was the only one who answered, but she was too sleepy to talk.

"Okay," I thought, "I'll call Dallas. I'm sure I'll find a screenwriter there. A professionally produced film would add credibility to my discoveries. But why work through a writer in Dallas? I should go right to Hollywood! Yes, that's what I'll do. I'll go to Hollywood. There, I will write my life story. I've led a fascinating life. I'll write it myself in Hollywood and then sell it."

The ringing of my doorbell jarred me back to reality.

Elizabeth was at my door. Sue had called and alerted her to my nocturnal phoning.

"Jill, how are you?" she asked with a concerned look.

However I answered that question convinced her that I was not well. Rather, I was manic. She pleaded with me to go to the hospital, but I declined.

"All right," she commanded, "I'm putting you under house arrest. For the next twenty-four hours, under no circumstances will you leave these premises." She handed me a tape recorder and a half-dozen tapes. "Instead of going to California, how about you dictate your life story from here? I'm coming back tomorrow. If you're not better, we're going in to see a specialist."

That seemed to be a reasonable compromise. As Elizabeth drove away, I fumbled with the controls on the recorder, settled back in bed, and began telling what I thought to be the captivating story of my life.

Telling the story of my life soon exhausted me. Lonely and feeling sorry for myself, I lay in bed, barely able to move.

After a few minutes, a manic wave lifted me high and I thought, "I'm about to become famous for my ability to see inside the brain. What should I wear when the media comes to interview me? The purple and black, pleated, two-piece hand-me-down from Beverly would convey an image of understated strength. Maybe I'll do my interviews in my windowpane jeans and flannel fur?"

Believing I had been favored for some unknown reason brought a stream of tears. I sobbed for awhile. Then I quieted myself, hoping my stomach pain would go away. I prayed for sleep that never came. Instead, my mania tormented me through the night.

The next noon, Elizabeth dropped in to check on me. Though I had no appetite, she opened a can of soup as we discussed the importance of eating to keep up my waning strength.

She left saying, "I'll stop back with Susie and Jane this evening."

During mid-afternoon, I made it to the kitchen without stopping to rest on the way. Weak from the exertion, I sat down on the church pew at my kitchen table and waited for energy to get out some crackers or cereal.

When I realized that energy would never come, I grabbed a can of 7 Up and headed back to bed thinking, "Elizabeth said it was important to stay hydrated."

Around six thirty, thoughts of visitors raced through my mind.

"The girls should be here by now," I thought. "Where are they? Did Elizabeth say seven thirty? Oh, who cares? They'll understand I'm too weak to entertain in the living room, but they can squeeze three chairs in this bedroom, and I'll be glad for the company. I haven't been out of the house, much less bed, all week. I wonder how long it will take the girls to notice I'm wearing my tap shoes?"

I found it reassuring to think that, if I died before they came, they would see that I croaked with my tap shoes on. I heard the front door knob turn. Not only did I have keen hearing, it was a small house.

Jane said, "She must be back in her bedroom."

Susie popped her head around the corner and asked, "What are you doing in that bed, girl?"

"What does it look like? I'm sick in bed. Thanks for coming," I said.

Elizabeth pushed a desk chair near my bed while Susie and Jane looked for chairs from the dining room. All settled, Elizabeth asked me to give them an update on my condition. I began a monologue that spoke of the predictable present before veering off in a direction that none of us saw coming.

I said, "Who was it who said we need to leave our past behind and move on to the future? I don't feel I should turn my back on my past. Instead, I'm going to step backward loudly while wearing these tap shoes."

With those words as my cue, I flung the covers from me and pointed my toe-tapping feet toward the ceiling in a dramatic voilà move. I sensed the girls checking their amusement in a collective pact to not encourage me, but I didn't care.

Following an hour or two of my nonsense, when the girls could stand it no more, they rose as one, hugged me, and slipped out the front door. I could hear their worried murmurings.

Only Elizabeth's words penetrated my garbled mind, "If you don't get your sleep tonight, we're getting you some medical help in the morning."

Heeding Elizabeth's warning and in desperate need of sleep, I took twenty-five milligrams of amitriptyline. Five milligrams usually guaranteed me a solid night. But the megadose had no effect. Elizabeth returned in the morning to see that I hadn't slept a wink. She convinced me that I should check into Summerhill Psychiatric Hospital, hoping that doctors there could help me regain my ability to rest. Elizabeth waited while I dressed. Later that day, she and Jane drove me there.

Normal people have no idea how difficult it is to voluntarily check into a psychiatric hospital. Though I had hundreds of weekly visits with therapists since the early 1970s and I had been hospitalized for a week with severe depression with catatonic features on my twenty-sixth birthday, I had never admitted myself. It was a line I feared crossing because I wasn't sure what I was about to experience. I knew that I wasn't me, but I wasn't sure if venturing forward would help me find my old self or if I would lose that person forever.

Built in 1988 in south Tulsa on forty-seven secluded acres of rolling hills, Summerhill featured wooded courtyards, walking trails, a waterfall, and a small lake. Their staff referred to it as a "campus." Everything about it was designed to present a retreat, resort-like atmosphere. They would have you believe that you were coming to relax.

Jane turned from the busy four-lane highway onto the winding two-lane road that led to the hospital. My body tensed as we drove along. As we crested a hill, we came upon a panoramic view of my destination, a complex of pinkish-red brick buildings. A man-made pond and illuminated fountains flanked the main building. At the main entrance, Jane stopped to let out Elizabeth and me and then continued on to park her car. Elizabeth accompanied me up the ten, broad-bricked steps that led to the impressive entrance door, the Summerhill monogram etched into its glass. With each step, my trepidation grew. I clung tightly to my overnight bag and pillow. As we entered the admissions area, I shook with fear. Try as they might to make this look like a vacation destination, I knew it wasn't, but I didn't know what it was.

During check-in procedures, my mania was in full swing. I squirmed in my chair, unable to get comfortable.

"Why are they talking so slowly?" I thought.

I knew where their sentences would end as soon as they uttered the first word.

"Come on," I thought. "Let's speed things up here."

If this were a race, I was well ahead of the pack. I was trying to be as pleasant as possible, but I had to squelch my impatience with these people who seemed so lethargic. I was a 78-RPM record being played at 33 and 1/3, and I continued to fidget in my chair.

Among the many questions asked of me, one included, "Are you suicidal?"

In my manic state, I didn't grasp the nuances of tense. I thought they were asking if I ever had been suicidal.

I replied, "Yes."

Though I didn't feel suicidal then, I inadvertently triggered an alarm that indicated I was.

The on-duty psychiatrist was at home, watching a football game. The admissions director called him on my behalf.

"Start her on lithium," he said. "And tell her that I will see her later."

In my condition, those words were the last straw. I couldn't believe my ears, and I became incensed. The Summerhill staff said the doctor had seen so many cases of mania that he could treat them sight unseen. I told them that I had never before experienced a case of mania and under no circumstances would I agree to take medication prescribed without being observed and examined first.

Elizabeth, Jane, and I left Summerhill with the agreement that we would possibly be back after the ballgame. Unbeknownst to me, the hospital staff advised Elizabeth and Jane that I should not be left unattended. Babysitting me had not been in their plans for the day, but they did drive me to my in-laws, Wally and Jocie Love. (Wally, a doctor, was the brother of Quint's first wife who had died of an aneurysm.)

Wally escorted me into his living room as Elizabeth and Jane backed down the driveway. I intended to tell Wally every detail of my dissatisfaction as soon as I could settle down. I called Wally my brother-in-law, even though he wasn't. But, in terms of the heart, he and Jocie held cherished spots in my patchwork of an extended family. Wally and Jocie could not have been more welcoming when Quint and I announced our plans to marry. Their two children were close in age to Brad and Mandy, and we made every effort for the kids to grow up knowing their cousins.

The focal point of Wally and Jocie's living room was an elegant, wraparound custom sectional sofa with many pillows that mirrored the color spectrum. Sitting in the middle of all that color made me feel regal. With Wally listening stoically in a chair across the way, it was almost like I was holding court. Jocie floated between the living room and the kitchen, replenishing the pot of spiced tea when needed.

Though I couldn't tell by looking, I was fairly sure Wally was marveling at how fast I was able to think. I whizzed around him on my own personal racetrack while he held the checkered flag in his lap, waiting for an opening that never came.

"Can you believe it, Wally? Dr. Outwater, the on-duty psychiatrist at Summerhill, had the nerve to diagnose and prescribe medication for me sight unseen just because he didn't want to miss any of the football game. I'm a Sooners fan, too, but there are times the job has to come first. And speaking of pleasure, it is certainly that for me to while away a Saturday afternoon with you and Jocie."

I spent the night with Jane. Sometime after three o'clock in the morning, I woke with my adrenaline racing. I was afraid to move, fearing I was going to explode. I asked Jane to come sit on me because I was terrified I was going to end up on the molding where the wall and ceiling met.

She said, "Jill, your eyes are totally dilated."

Sensing we were both scared, I offered, "If you will hand me the phone, I will try to get us some help."

I first called Elizabeth and pleaded, "Will you come?"

She countered with a question of her own, as therapists are wont to do. I felt I did not have the time or the energy to discuss the pros or cons of my request, so I hung up. My calls to Mieke (who had returned to Tulsa from Europe) and Maggie ended with the same result. Finally, I called Catherine, my last hope. She said she was on her way.

I gasped, "Thank you." I hung up, grateful I had at least two friends who would come with no questions asked.

To my surprise, all those I had hung up on came anyway. By the time Catherine arrived, so had everyone else. The story they all believed was that I was doing this to get attention. At the time, I knew Catherine, in particular, was angry, but I felt much too badly myself to care.

So back to Summerhill we went. This time, I noticed that the monogram on the front door of the administration building was also inlaid on the floor of its entrance. It was a large, green leaf. Because green was my favorite color, I thought this to be a good omen.

During pre-dawn on the morning of Sunday, November 8, I was admitted. I was escorted from the comfort of the fireplace and leather sofas in the visitors' area and taken through a secured room. We went back into a series of covered walkways that led to my unit. I noticed the industrial carpeting in the halls and common areas, which I thought must be there to muffle the cries of anguish from the residents. I was shown to a double room and introduced to my roommate, a woman about twenty years my senior with closely cropped gray hair in a tight perm. The deep wrinkles near her mouth and the bags under her eyes indicated she had not followed the regimen of preventive skin care that my mother espoused as imperative against the march of time. Mother was probably right about that one. The lady ignored me at first, and I was glad for that.

I sank onto my cot. Its mattress was hard as a rock. Camp Longhorn's beds were much more comfortable. Most patients received a spongy, eggcrate mattress to lay over the existing one. For some reason, I never did.

Sometime before dawn, my roommate shuffled to my bedside, poked me on the shoulder, and said, "Why don't you be quiet."

I didn't think I had been making any noise.

I thought, "Could she hear my thoughts? Did she hear me complaining about my mattress?"

She was likely just imagining that I was speaking out loud, but I agreed to be quiet, as she demanded.

In the darkened room, my awareness of time diminished. I focused solely on the staff's promise that a female psychiatrist would see me the first thing Monday morning. I naïvely believed she really would be at my side the first thing in the morning, as soon as she learned I was in desperate need of help.

Sunday passed slowly. I was uncooperative and unwilling to comply with any orders until I saw the psychiatrist. A medical doctor examined me, and he recommended that I continue taking my Bactrim.

On my inpatient psychiatric evaluation they noted my chief complaint was that, "I needed to get myself under control." During the night, I saw three overcoats and hats waving next to my bed.

As dawn broke on Monday, I tingled with the excitement that I would soon get professional help. The psychiatrist would help me put the episode behind me. With her guidance, we would lock the creature in a closet and throw away the key. By ten o'clock, she had not arrived. I became agitated and decided I could best contain my growing anger by getting under my bed.

Around eleven thirty, I heard footsteps entering my room. I saw shoes only a few feet from where I lay.

"Ms. Byrne, it's Dr. Gardier. What are you doing under there?"

My anger, humiliation, and embarrassment were too great for me to roll out immediately on request.

After a few moments of silence, I said, "Do you realize how difficult for me it has been waiting to see you?"

Rather than respond to my question, she ordered, "Join me in the room next door as soon as you feel ready for it."

Her voice was cold, serious, and distant. She reminded me of a female version of my first therapist, Dr. Breickman. It was not a pleasant memory.

Dr. Gardier was a rookie, a new psychiatrist on staff who had recently come from New York on a temporary assignment. I will never know why they assigned her to me. This was my biggest disappointment at Summerhill, realizing I was not going to get individualized therapy from an experienced professional. Catherine spoke alone with Dr. Gardier and told her that she believed I was orchestrating the entire episode in order to get an exemption from work. The doctor became convinced I was highly manipulative, and her position similarly influenced the rest of the Summerhill staff. During my stay, they viewed everything I said or did through that lens.

On my second day, I was moved from a double room to a single one close to the center of the ward. I was prescribed lithium along with several other medications, including mellaril and, of course, Bactrim. I felt miserable, and I mostly stayed in my room. Because of this, I missed many sessions where the rules were explained. One of the rules I missed pertained to dining privileges. Because I was considered a high suicide risk, a psychiatric technician accompanied me to my meals.

"What must I do to gain the privilege of dining unescorted?" I thought.

Others who came on the unit after me were eating by themselves. The rule I didn't know was that, if I shared my feelings in group, I could possibly go to the dining area unescorted. One day, the staff told me that I had earned that privilege, and I was thrilled. But after two meals, they told me that they had made a mistake. I evidently had not been speaking in my group session, and my solo dining privileges were being revoked. Upon hearing this news, I broke down and cried.

I attended two group sessions each day, which Patrice Allen and Lyn Lucas led. They were the social workers assigned to my unit. This attempt at therapy was not effective for me because I was hesitant to talk around people whom I didn't know. Besides, in group, the most manic patients spoke incessantly, and I found it excruciatingly difficult to concentrate on what they were saying. When I did try to talk, my thoughts raced much faster than I could express them, and it felt like my logjam of words and emotions might cause my head to burst. It was much easier all around to remain silent, but I wasn't aware that doing so was affecting my privileges. When the staff insisted, I went to the craft room and strung beads for a leather necklace. Mealtimes broke the boredom of the day.

To the Summerhill staff, I seemed to be just another imbalanced patient in the unit. They appeared too busy to listen, and they were likely thinking that anything I would say to them would be a manipulative attempt on my part. Only C.R., a tall, thin black man who was on duty at night, and Madelyn, a head nurse, listened. That was it.

During the week I was escorted to a separate wing of the hospital for a battery of psychological tests, the principal one being the MMPI, the Minnesota Multiphasic Personality Inventory. Developed in the late 1930s at the University of Minnesota, it is the most frequently used clinical test. It provides a measure of a person's problems, symptoms, and characteristics. The MMPI focuses on pathology, and it is nearly impossible for anyone to look well-adjusted on the profile.

I gave tests for a living, and now I was on the other side of the table. I knew my ability to concentrate was severely impaired, as was my ability to sit still. Nonetheless, I was marched through the procedure. The examiner made no effort to establish rapport during the first several hours of the test battery. Eventually, he gave me the MMPI to finish in my room and escorted me back to the ward.

One evening, I remember going to the on-duty nurse to report an extreme temperature contrast in the tips of my fingers. While we watched, beads of moisture appeared on my fingernails. I knew something weird was happening, and she just seemed to think I was hysteric. On the afternoon of Saturday, November 14, I began to feel waves of nausea and soon began to throw up. I was allowed to stay in my room for dinner and did not throw up again until late in the night.

The next day was a repeat. I somehow had the sense that staff members thought I was doing this in a manipulative attempt for attention. Physical distress was not readily dealt with in a psychiatric setting. By the morning of November 16, I knew I needed my own bed and bathroom more than anything. I had to go home, no matter the cost. The hospital staff agreed to place me on partial outpatient status, which meant I was expected to be there during the day, but I could return home for evenings and nights.

As required by this change of status, I was told my photo would be taken for an ID badge and I would need to have my lithium levels measured immediately at the St. Francis Hospital lab. They gave me my car keys to drive there. With effort, I made the trip. As I left the lab, I felt light-headed. Just out the door, I leaned against the wall and then slid down it to avoid fainting. Shortly, someone came by with a wheelchair and pushed me to the door. Still quite weak, I stopped a man who was driving a hospital maintenance truck and asked him to take me to my car.

Once there, I knew I would press on to my beauty shop. It was extremely important to me that I look as good as possible for this mental facility photo ID. I figured that, the bigger the hair, the better. When I arrived without a purse, the hairdresser worked me in and extended credit with no questions asked. By the time I returned to Summerhill,

I was aware that the act of driving was difficult, particularly stopping at lights. Later that day, I learned I would not be allowed to drive while on outpatient status. Though I was not happy with this news, I could see why it was in my best interest to comply.

At the time of my transition from inpatient to partial outpatient, hospital authorities called a meeting of my family of friends. Typically, immediate family members and close friends who live in the area are involved in these sessions. Family-wise, my mother, bound in a nursing home in Ada, didn't know of my hospitalization, and my sister in Dallas was dealing with plenty of her own problems. Therefore, my family representatives included myself, Elizabeth, Maggie, Catherine, Patty, an old friend from Ada who was an attorney. Dr. Gardier was supposed to be in charge of the session. Lyn Lucas was also in attendance.

The meeting, intended to help establish a plan of support for me, turned into an impromptu intervention. Catherine took charge of the meeting and spoke with the voice of authority. She articulately advised everyone to withdraw support from me because I had carefully orchestrated the entire episode in an effort to quit my job and draw disability. At the time, her actions hurt, but she had my best interests at heart. She felt I needed tough love. Elizabeth, my therapist, also received censure for failure to recognize my prepsychotic symptoms, which no one could delineate. The meeting closed with my friends advising me not to call any of them for help.

Catherine said to me, "If you need a ride, call a cab. You've got the money."

I knew I did not deserve this treatment, but I had neither the energy nor the mental clarity to attempt to defend myself. Through the years, my mother had made many cruel remarks. Only one did I believe to be totally untrue.

When I was in my early thirties, in a moment of frustration, she said, "Someday, when your friends really get to know you, they will give up on you. Maybe then you will finally learn that only your family is important."

As I looked around at my circle of friends, her words rang in my ears. My friends had given up on me.

"But if my family was so important, where were they now?" I thought.

That moment at Summerhill, I had never felt so alone or unloved.

As Catherine suggested, I called a cab. Soon, a shiny, new yellow taxi arrived. Imagine what was going through the driver's mind as he looked at me, a frazzled, middle-aged woman standing alone on the front steps of Summerhill with an overnight bag and pillow in hand. Silence filled the cab on the ride home. As we pulled into my driveway, I realized I had neither money nor my checkbook.

In my purse, I found thirty Disney Dollars left over from a recent trip that my sister and I had made to Disney World in Florida.

"Here," I said to the driver, waving the play money in his direction, "You will take Disney Dollars, won't you?"

He looked at me in amazement and said, "No, lady. I need real money, not Mickey Mouse stuff."

"Okay," I said. "Please wait while I run in the house and get my checkbook."

He agreed to wait. But my door was locked. I didn't have the key.

"I'll go across the street and call a friend," I said.

The cabbie replied, "That's fine."

He displayed a remarkable patience and understanding, something I desperately needed at that moment. He got out, grabbed a towel from the trunk, and began polishing the hood of his taxi.

I hurried across the street to my neighbor's house, knocked on his door, and requested to use his phone. I called Patty and asked her to bring my garage door opener. She seemed irritated to be bothered at work for such a mundane problem, but I did not care.

My neighbor, having no knowledge of my difficulties, but sensing my stressed demeanor, insisted I stay for tea. Two sips into it, I streaked out his front door and threw up in his prize azalea bushes. In time, Patty arrived. I unlocked my front door, got my checkbook, and paid the cabbie. I watched him pull away with the check and a high gloss.

For the next ten days, I arranged rides to and from Summerhill, often asking acquaintances for a ride and taking a taxi home. When I came home the night of November 25, I was distressed about how I would get through a Thanksgiving meal the next day. There was a new phone message from an acquaintance at work, saying I could call if I needed anything. I was so desperate that I called to ask if she would come get my prescription for suppositories filled to hopefully eliminate the possibility of throwing up on Thanksgiving at the Cooley's. She came with the prescription. (She later said that, upon seeing me, she feared I was near death.) That night, I finished my Bactrim prescription. That was also the last night I threw up.

Being somewhat up on consumer rights and having administered tests as part of my job with the Tulsa school system, I requested an appointment at Summerhill soon after my release to see my psychological test report. I was ushered to a room and handed my report.

The examiner, a Summerhill staff person, remained in the room, watching me intensely as I read. "Trying to read" would more accurately describe my effort because my mind was still reeling from my manic episode and the drugs. I focused all of my energy on one word at a time, praying I could get two consecutive ones to stick together and they would form some sort of image in my brain. But, try as I might, my eyes flitted randomly from word to word, over such phrases as "severe depression," "sense of hopelessness," "multiple personalities," "underlying bipolar disorder," "strong needs for attention and affection," self-punitive introspection," and "potential for suicidal behavior should be monitored."

The examiner in the room continued to watch me, and he began to shift impatiently in his chair.

"Shouldn't she be done by now?" he must have been thinking.

A phrase I recognized jumped out at me from the fog of sentences. Rather than joy at being able to understand a part of my report, I was sickened by what they said. I recognized them because I had written them time and again in my reports to describe students who needed help, that is, those students who I knew were on their way to nowhere. I knew them by heart.

"This woman appears to be functioning within the average to near-average range of intellectual ability."

Had I been standing, I would have dropped to my knees. I had always thought of myself as above average, but now I wasn't sure what to think. I closed the report and silently handed it to the examiner.

As I walked out the doors of Summerhill for what I hoped to be the last time, I noticed that, since my admission, all of the leaves had fallen from the trees. I shivered in the chill air. No, I never liked Novembers.

Desperate

As my mother languished mute and undemanding in a nursing home two years after the death of my daddy, my sense of urgency increased to dispel that ominous, dark cloud of depression that shadowed my enjoyment of everything. The years of therapy had been helpful, but it had been only to a point. My new internal mantra became "better is not enough." I realized my mother's impending mortality would soon free me to act on my suicidal ideation. The reestablishment of my base of friends had barely begun when I felt desperate to find a new therapist, that is, one who could rule me with an iron hand—one who would not let me get by with a thing.

In January 1993, I thought I found her. Dr. Samantha Wagner assured me she could handle people with bipolar disorder. She corrected me the first time I called her Samantha. "Call me Dr. Wagner," she said, establishing a professional distance. I guessed she was at least five years younger than I was. Dressed in a flowery shirtwaist dress that went to her mid-calf and wearing black leather heels, Dr. Wagner walked with her elbows out, which gave me the impression she was determined to handle a bipolar diagnosis.

Her office was on the fourth floor of a modern office building within a couple miles from my house. I could enter from the basement and slink off the elevator. It was the first door to the right. The waiting area was small. Stationed near a window, Dr. Wagner's receptionist sat in a compact space to the right. The doctor's office was down a short hall to the left. Four identical highback, overstuffed chairs were arranged in a square right in front of the door. I could tell which one was Dr. Wagner's because her legal pad, pen, and coffee mug were on the floor next to it. Over time, I tried the other three chairs, seeking where I felt most comfortable. My body type seemed ill-suited because the chairs projected my head forward. If only that had been my biggest problem.

We talked a lot about what I had done wrong and how I would need to adjust my attitude to embrace this bipolar diagnosis. She was clearly in charge of the session, which was okay with me because I desperately thought I needed a therapist who would take charge. Dr. Wagner seemed to feel sorry for Elizabeth and the difficult spot she believed I had put her in. Though Dr. Wagner and Elizabeth had only met over the phone, I sensed she liked Elizabeth better than me.

On some days, I could barely make it. My mind would not turn off, and I was so tired and confused that I didn't know what to do. I had nowhere to turn. I went to my mandatory bipolar group support meetings. They absolutely weren't working for me. I refused to celebrate my new mental status with those other highly medicated people. They were in the variable process of becoming comfortable with their bipolar diagnoses. I refused to accept my bipolar nature, but I kept attending the meetings as part of my compliance with professional treatment recommendations. Besides, I didn't have anywhere else to go. Most of the time, I just stayed in my place and paced until bedtime.

I called Dr. Wagner one day. Even though I had seen her two days before, as much as I hated to admit it, I was going to need another appointment before the weekend. She didn't really know me. She didn't know that I would never have asked for an extra appointment if I hadn't really needed it. Her secretary answered and put me on hold.

The next thing I knew, Dr. Wagner was on the line, saying, "Jill, this is Dr. Wagner. Do you really, really, really, really need to see me?"

"Did she want me to beg?" I thought. I hung up.

Dr. Wagner called right back and advised me to never hang up on her again. I couldn't find the words to reply. After several seconds of uncomfortable silence, she gave me the appointment. We met, but, by then, the session didn't do much for me.

I'll credit one major thing to Dr. Wagner. She supported my participation in a program that started me on my return to normalcy. I found an ad in a magazine called *Changes: The Magazine for Personal Growth* for a weekend workshop by Lifeworks to be held in Minneapolis. I very much wanted to go. The Lifeworks program director called to reject my application because my psychotic episode had occurred so recently. I asked Dr. Wagner to contact Lifeworks and convince them to accept me, which she did. They did under the conditions that I would adhere strictly to my medication and I would call Dr. Wagner each evening while driving to and from Minneapolis.

Before our first session, the director pulled me aside, warning me that, if I began to look the least bit manic, he would not hesitate to have me hospitalized.

After a brief lecture, our facilitator divided us into three groups. I was not assigned to his or his wife's group. I was put into a group of eight led by Mary, a soft-spoken, compassionate therapist. Over this intensive weekend, I participated in all of the exercises to my full ability, which dredged up a lot of my past in new ways. This was the first time I discovered the power of writing with my nondominant hand. Using my left hand, I wrote Mary a letter:

Dear Mary, I need your help I kno it's ok with u if I leave here w/ no visible sign of progress but it's not ok w/ me. I need relief and I want it now … Something you could do that might help is I need to hear I no longer need my strength all the time. She can't hurt me now and I don't have to hurt me for her … I'll B glad when I kno I don't hafta hide anymore. Your friend, Little Jill

New concepts were presented, such as psychological diastrophism and folie à deux (crazy for two). When the subject of secrets was addressed, I took it to heart when she said, "If you don't talk it out and work it out, then you'll act it out." Mary also told me the following things that were helpful:

Your mother was certifiably mentally ill. Your mother was a near-genius, and you are really smart. You are very creative, possibly with more talent than you know. Do you know you are generous? (I knew I had to admit this and wait to see what the trick was.) You have tremendous energy.

All of this insight impaired my sleep, but, with medication, I captured close to four hours each night. I knew that was the mandatory number of hours needed to stave off my lurking mania.

At the conclusion of the weekend, Mary approached me, took me by the shoulders, and said, "I believe you are going to write your story someday. When you do, I want a copy."

"Well, thanks," I replied. "But I can barely write my name."

My Therapeutic Piano

1993

I TOOK THE SCENIC ROUTE HOME, driving south at a relaxed pace along the Mississippi River, pondering all that had happened at the workshop and feeling pleased I had been able to complete it successfully. While driving, I thought about how envious I had always been of my mother's and sister's musical talents. Both could play piano by ear. When the two of them sat down together on the piano bench, their fun times really began to roll. I had nothing to contribute to their jam sessions.

In a moment of inspiration, it occurred to me that I could invent my own therapeutic piano as a way to begin to write out what was going on inside me. I decided to stop for a Coke and write down a few ideas for piano keys. The ideas were coming so fast that I hoped I could remember them long enough to write them down. I bought several pads of paper. I put each idea on the first page of a separate pad. I spread them around me as I sat on the floor. Each pad became a key on my piano keyboard. Excerpts from a few of my keys are as follows:

- **Key #1, The Rules:** Without hesitation, I penned the first rule. Appearance is everything. Additional rules came to mind, but they were each eliminated as I came to realize that the first rule overruled all other rules.

- **Key # 2, Glossary:** I listed words that had come up in therapy and had given me pause. "Generous" was the first word I defined. I listed every definition for the word found in the dictionary and then applied the meaning to my circumstance. For example, generous stresses the warm and sympathetic nature of the giver. When Mary told me that I was very generous, I didn't trust the compliment. What did she really mean? I might be generous, but what was I not? What was she holding back? The shame of not being able to accept a compliment had receded. In its place was quiet acceptance seasoned with a gentle pride.

- **Key #3, Messages from Home:** An excerpt from this key goes as follows. "March. And did I ever. I marched to my room. I marched back outside. I marched right back. I marched over here. I marched back to the store with the bread. I marched myself back home. I marched right back and picked it up. Ad nauseam." I still march. Between Summerhill in November and June, the sound of my march diminished to a tiptoe. When I returned from Minnesota, my march had the resonance of a hearty stomp, and a few toes were lost or wounded in the process. With the successful completion of this therapeutic negotiation stage, I believe the stomp will fade to a well-modulated pace for my life, saving the march for hopefully rare, appropriate occasions.

- **Key # 4, Get a Life:** When I hit that key of "get a life," I felt ecstatic. I believed I would. It was good idea, and it was better late than never. And when that initial rush settled down, I was left with the practicalities. It wasn't going to be easy. I was gonna need some help.

- **Key #5, When I Was a Little Girl:** When I hit that key of "when I was a little girl," I felt a soft sadness. Oh, how little Jill tried. What softened this sadness for me was that I received significant gifts of a little help along the way, though it was many years before I could recognize that help. When I was a little girl at 217 North Mississippi, I was put out on the back steps after my nap and given a bottle of Grapette. I remember being fascinated as I held the bottle up toward the sun and watched the different shades of purple change in the light. When I shook the bottle, the lavender foam matched my favorite hair ribbons. When I was a little girl, they said I used to cry a lot, but I didn't remember that. Another entry in this key is a story written in crayon:

Once upon a time, there were three precious little girls, each with a mother who was very strong in many ways. They were all sweet, cute, smart, and talented. Of all three little girls, Barbara was the sweetest and cutest, Lynn was the smartest, and little Jill was the most talented. They met in kindergarten. From that time, no matter who rocked the boat and for how high or how long, they were destined to float on the sea of childhood together. In the next twelve years, the boat never quit rocking. Lynn was at the tiller, Barbara was comfortably situated in the middle, and little Jill precariously balanced on the bow. With some predicted regularity, little Jill would become distracted and fail to maintain her balance. Frequently at these times, Lynn would bring the boat about, causing little Jill to scramble to recover but only to fall ceremoniously or unceremoniously into the dark, cold water. Her splash was sometimes so loud that everyone could hear, but, most of the time, she disappeared into the water so quietly that no one remembered she had even been there.

- **Key # 6, Gratefulness:** When I struck the key of gratefulness, I could feel my heart sing. The first entry in this key was simply, "Thank you, God."

Some of my imaginings of how I could play this piano may have possibly bordered at least on hypomania, but they still make perfect sense to me today. Using the piano metaphor as a therapeutic tool allowed me to balance difficult issues of negativity and self-doubt with positive aspects of my personality. Losing myself in the project made it easier to identify and face problems head-on.

Within an hour of returning to Tulsa from Minneapolis, I agreed to a blood test to determine my lithium level. I knew I was excited with the prospect my life could improve. Dr. Wagner figured my medication probably needed to be increased, considering my level of animation. Neither of us was able to reach my psychiatrist at Summerhill, which was especially upsetting to Dr. Wagner.

I entered our session with a newfound sense of liberation and my pillow. I was ready to cope as I plopped down on the floor with my pillow in my lap. I placed the white, sealed envelope on my left that contained the Richard Cory poem, my suicide note that I had kept in my office desk for nearly twenty years. I could see where my behavior could be perceived as expansive and manic, but I had returned with a plan. The first step was to be frank and honest.

"First of all, Dr. Wagner, for me, your chairs are all wrong," I said. I thought this would be a safe place to start before I addressed the suicide letter on my left.

"That's it," she snapped. "You are out of here. I don't have to handle this," she said.

She explained she did not have enough psychiatric support. And, for that matter, neither did I. I silently picked up my envelope. As I began to leave, I realized how poor the timing was, but maybe Dr. Wagner was doing me a favor. I would never have quit her.

While the piano theme had been predominantly in my thoughts on the drive home from Lifeworks, another idea that came to me on the road home from Minnesota was in response to Mary's challenge to look for opportunities to practice letting go.

Over the winter, someone gave me a jigsaw puzzle that was a jumble of steps leading nowhere in varying shades of dark blue and black. Though I prefer puzzles of landscapes, because it was a gift, I attempted it anyway. Besides, the dark colors definitely mirrored my mood, and the murky puzzle of a maze of stairs captured the dimness of my life. When I left for Lifeworks, the puzzle still monopolized my dining table with more than half still undone. As I neared Tulsa, it occurred to me that there might be a way to use this negative chore of driven compulsion to one of those opportunities that Mary was talking about.

Once home, I tore up the puzzle. Next, I selected a cut glass serving bowl and dumped all of the pieces in it. Then I grabbed a piece for each wastebasket in my house. As I dropped each piece, I gave conscious thought to let go of a different aspect of negativity in my life. I threw a couple pieces in my backyard to signify I could choose to do things differently. This serving bowl was placed on the coffee table in the living room. Each morning, I would put a couple pieces in my pocket to remind me to let go of difficulties I faced as I went through my workday.

This activity served me well. Now the remaining few pieces fit in a candy dish. I no longer need this exercise on a daily basis, but leaving it out is a reminder to me how far I've come. I literally threw out the darkness.

Before Lifeworks, I made notable progress in therapy, but it was rarely without a lot of dogged determination, and I was often on the edge of despair. I marked my experience at Lifeworks as the beginning step of a road to recovery.

A Piece of Paper on the Floor

1993

"WHO WANTS TO GO NEXT?" asked Elizabeth, the therapist who led our Tuesday night therapy/support group. Janet had just finished recounting her family's struggle in relocating her mother into assisted living. Marie began our session weighing the pros and cons of staying with her husband after he admitted his infidelity. I was so ready for my turn that I was about to pop. No one had seemed to notice that I intentionally dropped a piece of paper near the glass coffee table when I took my seat.

"I can't wait another minute," I said.

"Okay, Jill, why don't you catch us up on what you've been doing," Elizabeth offered.

"I just got back this afternoon from Minnesota where I attended a weekend workshop. I had so many good ideas bubble up on the way home that I had to stop frequently to write them all down," I said.

The look on Elizabeth's face appeared unusually guarded.

I continued, "When I talked with my therapist, Dr. Wagner, on my way home last night, she requested I go to the hospital lab first thing for a lithium level blood test before our appointment this afternoon. She seemed to mistake my enthusiasm for mania and says she doesn't want to work with me anymore. I may be wrong, but I think what looks like mania is just my newfound hope that my life can get better."

Delores and Shelly said "Tawanda" in unison as welcome encouragement.

I said, "One of my best ideas came to me on the drive home. I am building a piano of recovery, which won't make much sense tonight, but I'll explain it later. One of the keys of the piano addresses my role as a scientist. If you will hang with me, I need your help on an experiment."

My fellow members look intrigued. There is a question of mania behind Elizabeth's expression, but she is thankfully not interrupting me.

"I would like to go around the room," I said. "Each of you will tell me what you think when you see that object by the coffee table."

Each group member said, "There is a piece of paper on the floor."

"Now let me tell you what I think when I see the same thing," I said. "There's a piece of paper on the floor. I wonder how it got there? Is it important? What if someone thinks it's mine? Will they call me a litterbug? Did somebody drop it? Should I pick it up and look for a name? If I do, will they say mind your own business? Could it be a letter? If so, will someone be sad when they find it gone? I wish it were a letter for me. But then, they'd probably expect me to write them back. Should I turn it in? Where? Does everything have to be so hard? Maybe it is just a piece of paper on the floor. Why do you have to make such a big deal out of every little thing?"

When I finished, I said, "This internal dialogue is not uncommon for me, and it is an excellent example of how paralyzing many of my decision-making opportunities can become."

I instantly felt the innocent compassion from my group cohorts.

Elizabeth firmly wrested my turn away and said, "That must be hard to second-guess yourself on things that are not important. Sometimes, that kind of self-talk and the enthusiasm you have expressed tonight can be an indication of impending mania. I'm glad you had you lithium level checked today. You may need an increase in your medication."

Much to the surprise of all professionals concerned, my lithium level results came back within range. With this confirmation, my seed of hope broke through the surface. That was the summer I began to think differently.

My Next and Last Therapist

BACK FROM LIFEWORKS AND NO longer seeing Dr. Wagner, the only thing on my mind was finding a new therapist. After hearing of my lack of progress, Elizabeth suggested, "Why don't you ask Lyn Lucas if she would work with you? She would have psychiatric support at Summerhill. She knows you because she was assigned to your case last fall."

"I already did, and she said no," I said.

"Hmmm," Elizabeth said. "Would you like for me to call and check out the situation?"

"Would you?" I stammered at this unexpected gift of help.

With an earnest attempt at humor and a smile in her eye, Elizabeth replied, "It will cost you, and there will be no short jokes for the rest of the summer!"

"What could I say?" I thought. "It was a high price, but it was worth it."

"Thanks a bunch," I said.

Victory was confirmed later that day when Lyn called to schedule my appointment. What a relief! Exactly one month after Samantha kicked me out, I finally found someone I liked and who would be willing to work with me.

Armed with a boom box/tape recorder and the beginnings of my piano of recovery, I sprang to my feet when Lyn appeared and called my name. Her second-floor office was well-appointed. After Samantha's office setup, I was relieved to see lowback upholstered chairs. However, that day, I had every intention of sitting on the floor. I simply felt safer down there. Whaddya know? Lyn joined me! I was dressed for it. Poor Lyn was in a suit, hose, and heels.

I explained my reason for taping. I had become so tired of going through my history that, if this didn't work out, I would be able to give the tape to future therapists in advance and save my breath.

Lyn said, "Let it roll."

I knew I was talking as fast as I could. I was well-aware that time was money. She could go ahead and label me hypomanic, but I was mainly just in a hurry to get better. I finally believed it was possible.

Lyn listened well. Plus, she seemed interested when I laid out my piano keys. Near the end of the session, Lyn wrapped up by explaining the rules. They were rules I recognized as preceding my reputation of being difficult to work with. Though saddened, I was not deterred. By next time, I would be ready to discuss each and their impact for me.

I left with a sense that Lyn would be able to help me. Hope lightened my load. I pictured myself skipping as I took my stuff to the car. Next week, I would even be ready to confide my recent inability to read, something I had been too scared to admit to anyone.

I added several new keys while working with Lyn. One of them contained a letter to her:

Dear Lyn, Trust me. Deception played a key role in my survival, but my basic nature is not deceptive. As we all know now, the primary rule has been that I could only tell if someone asked. Please continue to ask. (You are off to a good start on this.) My theory is that, someday soon, it won't be as necessary, and we'll both know when.

Over time, therapeutically speaking, my piano of recovery worked well. It served as a natural incentive to work between sessions. Lyn joined the spirit of this framework by assigning specific keys when I asked for homework. I felt less alone the first time she put a star on my papers the same way a piano teacher rewards her beginning students.

Internal Integration

As 1994 PASSED AND MY mother's life waned, my drive to attain normalcy increased. If I did not find the missing pieces of the happiness that eluded me by the time her strange laughter was silenced in death, because I was such a fatalist, I would know then that my life could be no better and I would be free to proceed in ending it. The skills I had developed through individual therapies all helped, but I yearned for more. I began to search for an intensive treatment program beyond the Tulsa area. In the summer of 1994, I enrolled in a program called the Hoffman Quadrinity Process. It would provide me the hope that I so desperately needed.

I learned of the Hoffman program in an ad in *Changes* magazine. Most programs advertised were identified as treatment programs. Hoffman's description was different. Their eight-day program did not have the same emphasis on a medical model as the other ads portrayed. Hoffman was described as a retreat for anyone seeking to make lasting positive changes enhancing personal growth. They emphasized resolving family of origin issues through a highly structured program that had worked for tens of thousands, so I decided to give it a try.

The Quadrinity Process was first a theoretical model that Bob Hoffman formulated in 1967 and built on the framework that early childhood conditioning passes from one generation to the next in the form of a quadrininty (physical, intellectual, emotional, and spiritual). Bob's theory was that, if a person were wounded in any of these areas, he or she would pass those wounds on to his or her children. He believed the healing of those early wounds would serve to break the generationally instilled patterns.

Through the process, I learned my quadrinity was in a state of perpetual confusion. Physically, it was apparent I was a forty-eight-year-old, white female. Intellectually, I had achieved thorough under-standing of my early years through the years of therapy. Emotionally, I was subtly stuck at about age two. This is when I experienced signifi-cant trauma of abandonment and explained why, even as an adult, I categorized people with no more emotional depth than "someone is nice to me or mean to me." Spiritually, I had never gotten started.

Hoffman teamed up with a colleague in 1972 to present the quadrinity model along with something called the "negative love syn-drome" in group therapeutic settings. "Negative love" referred to the state of feeling unlovable. They stressed that negative love was not ge-netic. We adopted our parents' negative behaviors in the hope that they would love us if we were just like them, as vindictive revenge for not receiving consistent love and acceptance from them or to punish ourselves by compulsively acting out the traits that made us suffer and feel bad.

In order to derive the most benefit from the process, participants had to be willing to recognize that their spiritual self had brought them to that time and place for the purpose of finding the peace of mind, self-acceptance, self-forgiveness, and self-love that they had always yearned for. They had to accept that the emotional and intellectual aspects of their mind needed to surrender to the God-light part, that is, their spiritual self. I was ready to make that claim.

The process began before I arrived. In fact, I found the preprocess written assignment exhaustive. After reading a booklet on the negative love syndrome, there was a short-answer page to determine to what degree one understood the basic concepts.

Next, the assignment was to list my negative traits as well as Moth-er's and Father's. I identified nine for myself: controlling, stubborn, critical of self and others, ultrasensitive, phobic, self-conscious, sub-missive, insignificant, and ambivalence with attachment issues. I sailed through twice that for my mother. Some of which were critical, para-noid, fearful, consistently inconsistent, perfectionist, controlling, rigid, and reclusive. Only six came to mind for my father: passive, abandon-ing, submissive, loyal to a fault, heavy smoker, and chronic drinker.

We were asked to describe our parents' spirituality. Frances seemed to suffer spiritual conflict. An Episcopalian raised as a Baptist, she never seemed comfortable with either. Her spiritual search seemed to achieve little comfort for her. Though I'm not sure where Clifford was spiritually, he was a faithful churchgoer. Soon after he died, the priest told me I wouldn't believe the impact of his witness. Clifford spoke with his presence.

A final part of the preprocess assignment required composing a statement on how much I really wanted to be free of negative love. I wrote the following:

The prospect of becoming free of negative love is very inviting. I have been working for a long time to get to this point where I may feel safe enough to let go of the garbage I still carry. There have been a couple of other times I've felt equally as ready, but the window of opportunity was nailed shut. I am so incredibly tired of seeing negative aspects of my mother in myself. The potential relief I seek in surviving the Hoffman Quadrinity Process is major to me, yet I'm prepared to temper my internal enthusiasm as much as I need to keep my expectations in balance.

Commitment to the process was integral to each participant's success in breaking generational patterns. The decision to participate was not to be made lightly. Like many things, it was true that one got what one put in. If someone found the preassessment too much, then it was likely that the person was not ready to go through the process.

I arrived at the Hoffman session on a Friday afternoon in the summer of 1994. During the eight-day session, three teachers led our group of around twenty-seven participants. They assigned rooms and roommates. Then they met individually with each of us to go over our preassessment assignments. They privately pointed out obvious destructive patterns and challenged us to stay committed to the program, however difficult. Simple daily decisions were made for us, allowing us to remain focused on the bigger picture. The first issue I could not ignore was the lack of any partition between where the four of us slept and bathed. Modest among total strangers, I complained and did achieve the installation of a shower curtain.

My thoughts during the session turned to attributing my problems to my mother. It was soon pointed out to me that my daddy, however wonderful and dear, was not as squeaky-clean in my psychological abyss. In activities structured to look beyond the obvious, I came to recognize that my daddy was loyal to my mother to my detriment. For example, one day in the mid 1970s, my mother and I were having a discussion where she attacked every area of my life. Specifically, she reminded me how upset she was that I had squandered two fine teaching positions, choosing instead to study to become a counselor of all things. Then she tore into my being a divorcée who brought boyfriends home, none suitable to become a mate. (She said "boyfriends" with a sneer.) She continued by deploring my move to Tulsa.

"If you want to become a victim of big-city crime, well, that's your choice," she said.

And there was always the issue of my hair. It was either too short, too long, too frosted, too ratted, or too flat.

We had many of these discussions, but this particular one was especially brutal. My daddy was in the house throughout. At least once, he came through the kitchen where we were so engaged. He heard every word. Afterward, I rode with him to the post office. During the trip, I expressed how frustrating that experience had been and asked if he could agree with me that she was difficult.

His only comment was, "Jill, you must never say anything bad about your mother."

Not only would he not call her off me, he would not acknowledge her abusiveness.

On the sixth day, we participated in a lengthy meditation where my integration was instantaneous. In one melodious moment, all my parts (physical, intellectual, emotional, and spiritual) came together, and I sensed a congruency on an emotional and spiritual level as never before. I came to believe, without a shred of doubt, that there existed a higher power. Growth toward that moment had been coming for years, and there were several times I had at least momentary relief from my heavy heart. This felt different. I recognized a newfound security. Only time would prove the lasting quality of a sense much greater than relief. God was in my life.

As the Hoffman Quadrinity Process concluded, I decided to share my secret suicide letter, the Richard Cory poem. I asked the group to wait for me while I went to my car to retrieve the sealed envelope. I explained to them why I had kept the poem and then ripped the envelope and its contents into pieces before their eyes. There were no pangs of regret in disposing of something I had held as so essential to my well-being for nearly twenty years.

Our final exercise was to write a letter to ourselves and mail it home. Here is what I wrote:

July 14, 1994

Dear Jill, Let me be the first to congratulate you on having accomplished a very hard thing. Remember in May when you decided you needed a bigger push than traditional therapy? You looked at all the programs you could find and settled on the Hoffman Quadrinity Process, even though it was a little longer than you wanted. When you learned the price, you were staggered with second-guesses. Soon you regrouped and considered the expenditure equivalent to biking in Ireland for the same length of time. (Quite funny since you don't bike!) Commitment! Then the process homework arrived. Another golden opportunity to give up in a hail of 'Hell no!' Instead, you buckled down. It took a full week. Each day, you acknowledged you could not have done this a day sooner than you did. You left Tulsa and never looked back. Once in Wisconsin, you handled each disappointment and uncertainty as it came up and were never totally undone by not having a bathroom door! Then, in a room full of people, none of whom seemed someone you were eager to know, as the days grew, their faces took on significance, their beauty blossomed, and we were eventually united in a bouquet of many varied petals! But, most of all, you did what you came to do. You cried, and you got mad. Initially, fears hovered near when your mother's familiar voice was whispering, 'Jill, why all of a sudden do you think you can hit a pillow and raise your voice?' Then you were aware of this wretched person next to you doing just that. Each time, she was serving as a catalyst for you to let go of basic resistance. Later, during compassion, there she was again. Her crying gave you courage to join. And though you set your modern-day record of eighteen Kleenexes, you did not fall apart to the point you couldn't get your pieces back together. This is the essence of your victory. Thank you for taking that first courageous step. Letting each step build a cadence, you can march to for the rest of your life. You deserve the best, Jill

The Hoffman Quadrinity Process worked for me. I did not have to recant my story or listen to the stories of others. I became keenly aware of an internal physical shift. My muscular insides, which I held in a perpetually tense, alert posture, finally relaxed as I knew I no longer had to try so hard to hold myself together. Down deep, I knew I no longer had to try so hard about anything. It was really okay just to be. It was such a relief to feel softer and sense an unconditional love for myself for the very first time. I tempered my immediate excitement while I silently acknowledged and celebrated an internal calm I had never known. Only time would prove this true.

Final Communication

MOTHER LIVED IN THE JAN Frances Care Center from shortly before Daddy died in 1991 until her death in July 1995. Her four-year stay was nearly twice the average that most experience after admission to a care facility. What may have contributed to her longevity was her longtime commitment to healthy habits. Mother first became a health nut back in about 1968, long before healthy lifestyles were popular. At that time, she instigated a self-imposed exercise program of walking rigorously three miles, twice a day. She usually walked at the stadium track. She maintained this routine for at least twenty years. This was the most social activity she participated in the last quarter of her life, and many folks in town knew Frances as the "track lady."

The weather rarely deterred her. On winter days, she bundled up in a warm coat and sported her billed knit hat. With a safety pin securing a folded fresh Kleenex and a cellophane-wrapped peppermint to her collar, she headed out the door, much like a St. Bernard rescue dog ready for winter duty.

In conjunction with getting daily exercise, Frances switched to a healthy diet. She gave up all fried foods to prepare the likes of boiled cabbage and stewed tomatoes. She quit smoking cold turkey. She no longer had a mixed drink before dinner. Given this history, upon entering the Care Center, Frances had the physical conditioning of a woman in her sixties rather than that of the eighty-three-year-old she was.

During her entire stay, Mother never left the Jan Frances' premises on her own. Except for my Summerhill time when I was recovering from my psychotic break and unable to drive, I visited her regularly. The two-hour drive to Ada gave me ample opportunity to think through and make sense of our generational family issues.

Years before Mother entered Jan Frances, when it had been necessary for me to take an active role in my sister's legal commitment, she had told me she knew I would not hesitate to put her away as well. For years, she had obsessed about being placed in a nursing home. And that's what happened. Watching my mother deal stoically with her greatest fear may have been key in my beginning to develop compassion and a newfound respect for her.

For the first few months after Daddy died, Frances continued to dress herself each day, complete with tennis shoes, hat, and purse. When directed, she would play the piano in the reception area to the delight of the residents and staff. Once she asked me to suggest what I would like to hear.

I replied, "Tea for Two."

"All right," she replied and then enthusiastically launched into "Sentimental Journey." There were times early on when Mother wanted to go back to the way things used to be. She would approach the nurses' station as if it were a hotel lobby.

"Pardon me, I have had a nice stay here, but I need to check out and settle my account before going home," she would say.

"Well, Frances, Mr. Byrne has already taken care of your account, and you are paid up through tonight," the nurse would say.

"Oh, that was so sweet of him," Mother replied. With a gracious smile, she headed gamely back to her room.

The more she expressed her need to go home, the more the Jan Frances staff increased her medication. And sure enough, four months into her permanent stay, my physically fit, sure-footed mother was sedated to a point of imbalance resulting in an oft-dreaded fall. They say she did not cry and remained so calm that they didn't believe she had a serious injury. However, knowing her hip was broken, she fiercely refused all the assistance that was offered until emergency personnel arrived. My mother always said she would never survive a broken hip. After surgery, the doctors agreed, saying it was just a matter of time. They were so confident that they instituted no plan of rehab, but, Mother somehow lived on four more years after her fall.

Mother's accident coincided with my return from Jamaica. I had planned the trip for Brad and Mandy while their dad was off on his third honeymoon. On our last day there, Mandy and I had our hair braided. She had two tasteful narrow braids where I opted for a mass of beaded cornrows covering my whole head. As I went to visit Mother, hospital personnel stopped in their tracks to gawk at me, a middle-aged white woman bedecked in a mass of beaded braids. I knew my mother had lost her will to live the moment I entered her hospital room because she made no comment about my hair. After her hip surgery, Mother, wanting and waiting to die, refused food and water. Over the next two months, she gradually, yet reluctantly, began to accept both. Her healthy living left her in a stronger physical condition than her will to live. From that point on, from 1991 to 1995, Frances never initiated or participated in any social aspect of life. She conveyed total disinterest in current events, even a presidential election.

There were several occasions when she began slipping away. Even though do not resuscitate orders were clearly displayed, each time, the staff would make heroic efforts to bring her back. Maybe it was because she was a private pay. When I would arrive, her eyes would plead, "Please make them quit saving me." Her body had just simply outlasted her will.

Whenever I visited Mother, her eyes conveyed a look that she was glad to see me. There was no scold in them for not coming to Ada more often. Mother's eyes came most alive when Beverly made her less frequent visits. On those occasions, Beverly and I shopped together for Mother and sometimes found something identical for all three of us. Mother seemed to notice, but she generally didn't care about our attempts to relate. We could tell she was always interested to see Beverly, but she seemed to recognize I was the one she could count on in the end after all.

I have only one photo from my mother's nursing home days. It is not of her, as it would have robbed her of the dignity to be photographed in a place she could not escape. The photo is of the window by Mother's bed. She had crumpled back the Venetian blinds enough to see outside. The picture reminds me of her desire to see the world on her terms, limited as they were, neither seeking favors nor waiting for someone to help open the blinds and extend her view.

Though Mother stopped talking after her broken hip in May

1991, I never knew for sure whether she was unable to speak or just preferred not to. I always had a sense she knew who I was and understood what I said. On July 13, 1995, my phone rang at five o'clock in the morning. The nursing home in Ada was calling to tell me that my mother had died. While I heard the words, my internal reaction felt hollow as I began to make her funeral arrangements.

After Lifeworks, I tossed away pieces of a jigsaw puzzle to symbolize letting go of my life's difficulties. I had saved a few pieces of the puzzle for the occasion of Mother's death. At the funeral home, I handed the puzzle pieces to my niece and asked her to place them in the casket with Mother as a symbol that the major source of negativity in my life was now gone.

Like Daddy, to the end, Mother never asked for help. This was one of the differences between us that I still celebrate. Learning to ask for needed help was a key in breaking through my life of depression.

How ironic I was cured of depression at Hoffman exactly one year before Frances died. In the spirit of all things happening in perfect timing, that last year gave me the window to tell Mother that I held no resentments. While she had always despised the idea of me receiving any therapy, it had been the vehicle for me to learn she had done the best she could. I was taking that best to finally do the best for myself. Occasionally, there were tears in her eyes as I made my peace with her. I feel strongly that I have a much more engaging and vibrant relationship with my mother now than I did when she was alive because her critical voice has been silenced.

I recently ran into the department director who hired me into the Tulsa Public School system in 1974. Over the years, I often sensed she regretted hiring me, so I was greatly amused when she leaned over and whispered to me, "I never thought you would amount to this much."

Those were my mother's sentiments exactly.

Bactrim

1995

ON JULY 4, NINE DAYS before Mother died, I awoke early with a familiar abdominal discomfort. The on-duty emergency room physician diagnosed my second attack of diverticulitis. Bactrim was again the prescribed drug of choice. After the holiday weekend, my regular gastroenterologist saw me. Though my initial symptoms had subsided, the test result of blood in my urine puzzled him.

Five days later the test results were unchanged, and my ability to function had begun to deteriorate. I initially attributed my general malaise to scorching summer heat. Each day, I struggled to continue through my scheduled day while sensing the waning of my life force. In the midst of my own health problems, Mother died.

When the clinic receptionist offered me an appointment with a urologist three weeks out, my patience dissipated.

"My mother just died," I said. "If I am not seen today, there will be a double funeral."

There was a long pause. The receptionist finally said, "He will see you this afternoon at two o'clock."

The doctor appeared to be in a big hurry and didn't even look at me. He studied my chart, which included notes on my psychiatric hospitalization a few years back.

He then confidently announced, "There is nothing the matter with you. You are just having a classical hysterical reaction where you think your body is in pain, but, in reality, it is not."

With metered strength, I left his office for the funeral home two hours away. There was no energy to question the doctor's diagnosis, yet his pronouncement did nothing to relieve my physical discomfort.

Moving from the car to the first vacant chair in the funeral home, I was happy to see my Dallas family had already arrived.

My nephew Blane's wife, Janis, came right up to me and said, "What is the matter with you?"

I repeated what the doctor had said.

"Your face is flushed. You have red streaks on your arms. Let me see your stomach." With a confirming quick glance, Janis said, "Whatever medicine you are taking, you are deathly allergic to it, and you should stop it immediately."

The on-call doctor concurred with Janis.

In the next month, as my general physical well-being improved, I began to think through the comparisons of this aborted psychotic episode with the full-blown one in 1992 and supposed the two were connected. The interaction of the antibiotic Bactrim with Prozac in1992 and lithium in1995 led me to theorize that my psychiatric experience was more possibly due to a severe allergic drug reaction than an accurate debilitating bipolar diagnosis.

I began to gain a clearer understanding of sleep as the gatekeeper of mania. There were numerous times when that sleep gate was inexplicably left open and I teetered toward psychosis. Once a brain takes off on this alternate path toward mania, it doesn't matter what pushed it down that path. The brain stays on this pathway, and its owner becomes locked in a manic pattern. I resolved to ensure a minimum of four hours sleep per night, working toward at least four uninterrupted hours. Attaining that benchmark did not happen overnight, but I finally reached it. Over time and through deep sleep, my newly wired brain pathways gradually healed. Through hard work and extremely good fortune, I was able to prevent a psychotic episode recurrence during that precarious first eighteen months of my brain's recovery.

A light in my tunnel of mental illness darkness began to flutter. My current therapist, Lyn, and I started to consider reframing my whole experience since November 1992. When I approached her with my interest in seeing if I could get off the possibly unneeded lithium, she respected my decision to try, though she certainly did not share my enthusiasm. The prescribing psychiatrist offered only the foreboding prediction. If I stopped taking lithium, I would have even a worse recurrence needing rehospitalization within one year.

I still believed I deserved the chance to pursue my theory and realized I had the most to gain or lose in the effort. I pledged to Lyn that I would agree to vigilant monitoring. If my hunch was wrong, I would not hesitate to reaccept the diagnosis and lifelong prescribed medication. On that August date, we agreed, as a precaution, to not begin the experiment until after Mandy's wedding in January.

The gradual tapering off lithium began on February 1, 1996. By the end of March, I reported to the psychiatrist all the welcomed improvements I had noticed, including no hand tremors or skin rash. Most significantly, I had regained my balance. For the last few years, I noticed I held on and went no higher than the first step on a ladder. Nor could I stand on a street curb without teetering off balance. I had chalked up this to the old age of forty-eight.

The psychiatrist countered, "Why didn't you tell me about your loss of physical balance?"

"You never asked, so I didn't think it could be related to medication," I replied.

"Well, that symptom is certainly an indicator of drug toxicity," she said.

Within the same month, my financial advisor commented, "I don't know what's different with you, but you suddenly seem to understand what I've been trying to get through to you for the last few years."

As I continued to experience physical and mental improvement off lithium, others remarked on this positive change. Lyn and I agreed I would contact the new director of Summerhill Psychiatric Hospital and see if he could provide any supportive studies for my theory.

The six weeks I had to wait for my appointment was an appropriate test for manic depression, but I simply waited with no disastrous results.

The director listened well during my May appointment and offered to study the literature and get back with me. He did and said he found no studies about antibiotics causing psychotic episodes and resulting in bipolar diagnosis. He believed my experience justified documentation and suggested we file it with the FDA. We submitted my written account and letters of support from him, Lyn, my therapist, and the prescribing psychiatrist.

Though I never received the anticipated thank-you note from the FDA, I felt a degree of satisfaction when Jane Pauley went public with her book, *Skywriting: A Life Out of the Blue.* I believe her bipolar disorder was correctly diagnosed as being triggered by a drug reaction because, along with others, the information I contributed in a small way broadened their criteria for the disorder.

Magshots

"WE HAVE PUT OFF YOUR birthday party long enough. Come on over to Elizabeth's for a dress rehearsal. Be there at two, and bring some of your sister's dresses."

I hung up the phone with Jane, wondering just what they had going on. My birthday had passed unheralded three weeks earlier on January 12, 1998, and I was beginning to lose interest in celebrating, as they obviously had.

My friendship with these three, Elizabeth, Jane, and Susie, had been born ten years earlier out of supporting each other through our various personal and tragic difficulties. We found that our impromptu late-night gatherings allowed us to share grief through life/death situations. By the end of each evening, much lighter topics were savored with sidesplitting, healing laughter. We were not amused when a male friend referred to us as the "Mafia." Preferring a softer image, we dubbed ourselves the "Magnolias." But could four diverse and opinionated women manage to travel together?

Our first travel weekend was an experimental trip all the way to the horse races in Oklahoma City. We left Tulsa on Friday afternoon, where it was seventy-two degrees. By the time we checked into our hotel that night, it was twenty-eight degrees and snowing. The next morning, we plowed on to the races. We were studying our tip sheets when they announced all races were cancelled due to inclement weather. We hardly noticed as our party laughed on. The normally hour-and-a-half trip home on Sunday took Jane, our most accomplished driver, around five hours. Again, no one cared as we enjoyed the continued levity of our newfound friendship.

Ten years later, I was still laughing as I entered Elizabeth's expansive bedroom that had been transformed into four dressing stations. Each station held an assortment of dresses, scarves, shoes, costume jewelry, and shawls. A pile of hats on Elizabeth's bed was available on a first-come, first-serve basis.

"Remember the water color portraits of four women in hats you gave us for Christmas?" Jane asked.

"We have an appointment to have our picture taken in similar dress next Saturday," Susie offered.

Elizabeth added, "We have had to change the appointment once because of Susie's trip and once because the photographer got sick. Sorry we kept putting you off. You probably thought we didn't care."

"It's gonna happen," Jane chimed in.

And so it did.

"You girls are hilarious! Do you always have this much fun together?" Dwight, the Motophoto photographer, asked while trying unsuccessfully to maintain a straight face.

He had his hands full as he tried to corral postures and expressions from the four of us. It was no small task, especially when someone was usually trying to upstage, always to the amusement of the remaining friends.

Dwight himself was a new piece of our amusement. Though he didn't offer why, he was clad in a partial body brace. He seemed to be the type that attracted misfortune. When he stepped off a small footstool, one of its legs collapsed. He caught himself as we girls gave a collective gasp. He offered his low-ceiling darkroom as a place for us to change into street clothes for a regular photo while we were there.

"Dwight, there's no mirror in here," Susie announced.

He soon knocked on the door, holding the remains of a four-foot-high mirror with a jagged edge. As he squeezed in to set it in place for us, the broken edge pierced a hole in his ceiling. No one dared ask how many years of bad luck he already had, but we all wondered under our breaths.

After Dwight captured the predetermined number of photos, he said, "Y'all are so much fun! Do you mind if I go ahead and finish this roll?"

Who could say no to that offer?

The mix of friends egging each other on and a photographer eager to seize the moment contributed to a magical time for all.

Another roll of film later, Dwight said, "Y'all crack me up! My photographic specialty is dogs, but, if you'd come back next week, I'd like to enter you in a contest."

We arrived the following Saturday with dishes and petit fours as Dwight was setting up the stage. He had selected a large, tan piece of paper for our background. As we stood there, he literally nailed that piece of paper into the back of an old upright piano. Like magic, our tearoom setting was complete. We devoured the petit fours, laughed our way through the photo shoot, and then left with our load of props.

A few days later, we went back to pick up the pictures. Ten photos were part of our purchased package. The other one hundred and ten were on the house. I shared my favorites at my office, and people got a kick out of them.

Gunda, a fellow co-worker, was quite serious when she came in my office and said, "Jill, these could be greeting cards. I really believe you should pursue it."

From that point on, Gunda was the strongest catalyst of encouragement that Magshots ever had.

The name, Magshots, came easily. So many close-ups of the Magnolias resembled mug shots, so Magshots seemed a natural name with the added moniker, "dressed-up greeting cards." Dwight readily signed over all rights, including negatives, and expressed his enthusiasm.

He said, "You girls take this as far as you can go."

Because Judy in my Sunday school class worked in a popular card shop, I asked her to look at my photos. I told her I was open to any suggestions she might have in how to proceed. Without hesitation, she recommended I come by the store and talk to Christine, the card buyer.

Elizabeth went with me to meet Christine. The barest of introductions were exchanged while the card pro rifled through our huge stack of photos. We had to look closely to spot any change of expression in her reactions to our pictures. In fact, Christine never actually gave us any positive encouragement, yet the fact she droned on for forty minutes about the difficulties and pitfalls of entering this highly competitive industry was encouraging in itself. We left with guarded optimism.

Again, I fell back on an oft-used lesson I had learned in therapy. When confronted with indecision at one of life's forks, do the next most obvious thing. Following leads to find resources for publishing took a while, but, as soon as I met Roy, the gruff, old owner of his printing company, I knew we were a fit. Without going overboard, he counseled me through the production process and instilled a confidence in me that our project had merit.

My own enthusiasm was on fire, which, with my mental history, may have seemed like a red flag to the other Mags. While it was not unusual for me to come up with creative ideas, I had no track record for independently sustaining my efforts to a productive conclusion. Certainly, without Gunda's daily urging, I would not have had the confidence to continue in my newfound entrepreneurial efforts. The girls made it clear that they enjoyed our photo sessions, but they were unwilling to join me in the day-to-day trials of a start-up business.

Jane was the only Magnolia with even a whit of business experience, so it is no wonder that the other two were hesitant to believe or recognize the potential inherent in this accidental project. As soon as our first four cards rolled off the press, I was faced with our first production mistake. I had ordered our cards too large for our envelopes. A quick trip back to the printer afforded a recut for a nominal fee.

Elizabeth accompanied me for the initial launch into local retailers. While a prominent local bookstore turned us down without a look-see, a local gift store, Jan Markeys, took the plunge. We had our first sale and garnered sixteen dollars. Near the end of the first day, a retailer commented our line was cute, but she would not be interested until we also offered some cards that were "on the edge." Once we doubled our line and included two with a double entendre inscription, we landed her account.

Ten months after our first sale, our line had grown to fourteen images. On President's Day in 1999, I sold Magshots to nine out of ten local retailers I approached and collected two hundred dollars in sales.

Only Gunda matched my excitement. The Magnolias acknowledged my perseverance by presenting me a plaque for "Saleswoman of the Year." We were on a roll.

Appearance Was Everything

A FTER BEVERLY FINALLY GOT IN touch with her anger, she poured out all of her regret with alcohol, often splashing it on family and friends until she reached her nightly goal of oblivion to stop the pain. She would awake before dawn, put herself back together, and trip off to work with a happy face, none of her co-workers the wiser. This went on for her last eighteen years. One day in August 1999, around six o'clock in the morning, with her first drink near the bathroom sink, her body quit as she was in the middle of hair prep.

The autopsy determined heart failure to be the cause of her death. The scientific part of me wished the autopsy could have provided more information on how she ticked than how she died. To me, she had always been mysteriously wonderful. I often studied the various facets that contributed to her popularity.

Are we born with poise? If so, she got it all. There is a fine line between being outgoing and overbearing. For the first half of her life, she never crossed that line. Beverly met no strangers. People young, old, rich, or poor were drawn to her. With every interaction, she had a gift of connecting with each on a personal level, shifting the attention on them and away from herself.

Ellen Bumpers commented, "Jill, we always thought you might end up in a mental institution someday."

I didn't share the rest of her sentence, which was "but we certainly never thought Beverly would have serious problems." She said this the day after my niece, Gail, and I went to court to commit Beverly for the first time.

Beverly succeeded in pleasing Mother until she, at the age of twenty, married Bob. Then without a hitch, she pleased him until she was fifty and couldn't do it anymore. People thought they were perfectly matched. She put others first naturally and without a thought. He thought only about himself and how everything reflected on him.

Beverly mastered our mother's mantra of "appearance is every-thing." It governed her long after it didn't matter anymore.

Years before she died, Beverly told me, "There is only one thing in this house that may be of real value. If anything should ever happen to me, I want you to have it."

She was speaking of a seventeenth-century Russian icon that hung in her den, just below an old mirror encased in ceramic brown lattice with green ivy. A friend of Beverly's had purchased the piece on a trip to the Ukraine. To my untrained eye, the ceramic mirror appeared the work of a rank beginner. On the other hand, it was evident the icon had once been a work of exquisite beauty. Placed on a slightly bowed panel of wood, roughly nine inches by twelve inches, were figures of Jesus and two angels with him done in intricate patterns of copper and tin. The frayed halos curled away from the board, highlighting the delicate faces painted on the wood. Everything about the piece spelled "antique."

After discussion with Blane, Beverly's son and executor, we agreed I would have the icon and mirror appraised sometime down the road. The road shortened considerably when we heard that "Antiques Road-show" would be coming to Tulsa in midsummer. Tickets would be available at noon on the Saturday of Memorial Day weekend. At twelve sharp, I dialed, prepared to speak with someone associated with the show. When a recording answered, I panicked and hung up the phone. I quickly regrouped and tried again and again for the next hour with no success. Though I had never ordered anything over the Internet, desperation forced me to give it a try. Four tickets arrived in the mail a few weeks later, which I took as another clear sign I was moving in the right direction.

Judiciously dispensing my three remaining tickets, I gave one to my neighbor and friend, Elizabeth, and we made plans to go together. Several friends came to view my treasure, and I cautioned all not to get too close. The frayed metal appeared fragile, and the oil from our skin might somehow tarnish and cause further deterioration. Elizabeth's daughter also came. As president of a local antique club, she was duly impressed and asked if I had any other antiques. I brought out that old mirror, which she immediately identified as Majolica. She insisted I also take it along for a professional look-see.

As the time neared, my expectation of being discovered soared. Beverly's icon and possibly the mirror would surely catch the eyes of highly skilled appraisers, probably setting me apart from run-of-the-mill collectors.

The show began at noon, so, that morning, I had time to have my hair done; don my chocolate brown, brushed silk pantsuit and black flats; bolt down a light lunch; and pack a small cosmetic bag for the green room before Elizabeth picked me up. The icon was packed in a borrowed ice chest that I strapped to a dolly. The mirror was secure in a small, rolling flight bag.

As my momentum built, I alerted Beverly's three children that good fortune was just around the corner. Should the icon exceed five digits in value, I would call each from the floor of the convention center to confer about an instant college fund for Beverly's six grandchildren.

Inside the Tulsa Convention Center, Elizabeth and I rolled our treasures in a constantly moving line for the next three hours. Shortly after three o'clock, we parted to wait the moments of discovery in our respective specialty areas. Forgotten were my tired legs and sore feet as I gingerly unveiled the icon and placed it in the appraiser's hands. I stepped back with bated breath ready to capture his ah-ha moment as he realized the significance of such a rare find. While bent over the wood, he motioned me nearer.

He asked, "Do you see these small holes around the edge?"

"Yes," I said, nearly bursting with pride.

"Obviously, the frame that was ripped away was worth much more than the icon itself. Still, I suspect you could get one or two hundred dollars for it," he said.

His voice faded away as he turned to the next person in line. With a gentle Frisbee flick of the wrist, I returned the icon to the ice chest and trudged on to the Majolica area. That guesstimate was three times the worth of the icon, but it was no consolation.

I hope Beverly enjoyed the irony as her little sister shuffled off for a margarita on a hot summer Saturday wearing her Sunday best.

Celebrity Status

B Y THE END OF 1999, there were twenty-eight images in the Magshots line. A showroom in the Dallas Market picked us up in time for their buying season beginning in January. I prevailed on the girls to come with me to Dallas for the first weekend of the show. We parked at the Anatole Hotel across the Stemmons Expressway from the Trade Mart and changed into our Magshots outfits in an Anatole restroom. No sooner did we climb on the shuttle bus, we had everyone's attention, and a couple of retailers asked for our autographs.

A gentle mob surrounded us as we stepped out of the bus. Retailers are always on the lookout for something new. In our dated garb, we attracted more attention than any of us had expected.

We made our way to our showroom and were promptly introduced to two artists from Wisconsin who were interested in meeting with us during lunch. Though the food court was packed, the six of us descended on one centrally located empty table. Many heads were turned as we settled down to talk business.

Out of the blue, a woman shrieked, "There are the Magshots! The Magshots are here!"

This woman, a retailer in an Oklahoma City suburb, had been carrying our line with excellent results and several reorders since the previous summer. Strangers soon approached our table, seeking information for the location of our showroom. It was all heady stuff, especially for the other three Magnolias who had their doubts where this could go.

Even my misadventures turned out positive on a sales trip in Tennessee. By this time, I had developed a sales strategy that significantly reduced my exposure to rejection. In fact, it secured a successful sales rate around 90 percent. I got off the interstate and drove on old highways that went through small towns. I learned not to rely on my best judgment in sizing up a retail sales opportunity. Instead, I looked for neutral businesses, such as abstract offices, banks, and chambers of commerce. I introduced myself and asked for directions. At no time, did anyone refuse an invitation to tell someone where to go.

I showed them a few cards and asked if there were a retailer of any kind in their community whose humor was similarly a little bit on the edge. Without exception, someone could provide me a short list of storeowners.

I would then walk in the first store on the list and say something like, "Mr. Hill over at the bank suggested your humor might be a good fit for my little line of greeting cards."

It was also to my advantage that I could fill their order out of the back of my car, thus saving them shipping charges. It was fun to track back to the bank and present "Mr. Hill" with a complimentary card and tell him he had been right. I could often be in and out of a town within an hour.

This was the case as I drove down Highway 64 in the fall of 2000. I sold at the first stop in the first three towns on my route. Each town was roughly a thirty-minute drive to the next one. By the time I stopped at the town square of town number four on my list, I became acutely aware of hunger and beginning fatigue. Having passed up a lunch stop earlier, I figured I would look for a bit of ice cream to tide me over until dinnertime.

When I reached for my designer pocketbook, a gift from Beverly, it was not there. I had no memory of seeing it since I checked out of the motel first thing in the morning. My momentum was now gone.

Explaining my plight to the women in the county clerk's office in the courthouse, one woman offered to use her cell phone to call the store that bought Magshots in the third town. They reported no sign of my wallet. Unsure of what to do, I decided to begin to retrace my route.

Back in the third town, I located the police station and went in to report a missing wallet. An officer interviewed me at length and offered me his business card in case I should later be stopped.

"Fat chance," I thought.

My driving record was close to impeccable. We discussed my need for gas before returning to the second town. The officer gave me the locations of two convenience stores where management might be willing to accept my out-of-state check for gas without identification.

The employee at the second station I tried called his manager and gave me the phone to plead my case. I must have sounded trustworthy enough because, before he hung up, he offered that I include a fountain drink with my gas bill.

So, as the sun began to set, I headed back west and reflected on this four-lane highway through hills and valleys. Visibility was unrestricted, and traffic was sparse.

I remained relaxed and felt assured I had not been given more than I could handle. This was still true when I saw the highway patrol flashing lights behind me. In fact, I figured they might be stopping me with good news regarding my lost pocketbook.

Even with this thought in mind, I innocently asked, "Officer, have I done something wrong?"

"Yes, ma'am," he replied. "I clocked you going sixty-seven in a fifty-five zone."

"Officer, it's a long story," I said.

My composure cracked as I began to explain the absence of my driver's license. It wasn't until he asked for my name did I begin to cry. He radioed the name I gave him.

The voice from the squad car blared, "There's nobody by that name registered in Oklahoma."

I explained, "My divorce finalized before I ever got around to changing my name on my license."

I waited for the officer to straighten things out.

When he came back to the window, the patrolman leaned in and said in a thick Southern drawl, "You're just havin' a bad day. Go get some rest, and start over tomorrow."

Licenseless, yet ticketless, I drove on to the second town I'd stopped in earlier. Finding the same small motel chain I had stayed in the night before, the office staff offered to call their sister motel and get my credit card number from them.

Once checked in my room, the phone rang. It was the front desk inquiring whether I had had any dinner. In response to my negative reply, I was sent across the street to Subway, where I was instructed to give my tab to the motel front desk. Back in my room, I heard a knock on the door. The manager handed me a can of Coke, saying I hadn't ordered a drink.

Shortly, I recovered enough to think to call my neighbors in Tulsa to check my answering machine. Sure enough, there was a message from the daughter of a woman in the third town. She had found my wallet in the grass by the courthouse on the town square. I remembered sitting on a wall there to write up my invoice. She turned the wallet into the police. The next morning, I gratefully picked it up and then drove straight to their weekly newspaper office to take out a public ad of thanks. A clerk instructed me to save my money. She had me just sit down and write a letter to the editor for free, which I did.

Parts of the addictive aspects of my personality are visible when I am on the road marketing Magshots. Once in the selling groove, it is most difficult to stop. It's always "one more store."

Before driving back to Tulsa after selling cards in the Dallas area, I decided to make one more stop in Frisco, Texas. The store owner's humor was a perfect fit. When she quit laughing, she said we needed to be in a market showroom.

She said, "In fact, Rudy Camacho's showroom would be ideal."

I had approached Rudy a couple years before. When he offered to show our cards, I chickened out. I didn't think we were ready for the big time. Five minutes later, the owner excused herself to answer the phone. It was Rudy Camacho calling. As I heard her describing our cards, I could imagine his lukewarm response when he figured out the small line she was talking about.

I heard her say, "Let me know, Rudy. If you are not going to take her, I'll find a showroom that will. I am buying her cards before she leaves my shop today."

When I got home, I had a very friendly message from Rudy, saying he had checked his records and noticed we had last talked in July 1999. He was interested in seeing how our line had grown. Arrangements were made for me to bring Magshots to the New York Stationary Show so he would show them in his temporary booth there.

My friend Lynn from grade school days lived in Manhattan and invited me to stay with her. She even rode the bus out to LaGuardia to meet me. We traveled around together on public transportation or walked. The first day I kept up with her, but she was in better shape than I. All the bones in my lower body screamed with each shuffled step.

The next morning, I was to meet Rudy at the Javits Center. He advised me to bring a couple boxes of my cards and all the promotional materials I could carry on the plane. I enlarged and laminated some photos at Kinko's to suffice for promo signage and juggled all this into a cab for my first solo ride in New York City. Because I was alone, I chose to ride in a quiet style and not chat as I often do.

Upon arrival, I hurried into the cavernous entrance of Javits and went to the registration area to learn where I could find Rudy's booth. I was the first to arrive. Forklifts were chugging around everywhere, so I sat at a small table to wait. A woman stopped in and said her name was Cynthia. She wondered if I had seen Rudy. We talked a bit. When she asked, I showed her a few Magshots before she rushed back upstairs.

About the time Rudy arrived, it occurred to me that I must have left my missing signage from Kinko's in the cab. Reluctant to tell Rudy, I was plotting how Lynn might help me reconstruct something that night when, about an hour later, two handsome New York state troopers in Stetson hats appeared at our booth, asking for Rudy Camacho.

We both looked astonished. Then I noticed they were holding the signs I had left in the taxi. The cabbie had returned them, and the show officials had asked the troopers to find their owner. With no ID on them, of all the people in the Javits Center, these troopers had run into Cynthia two floors above, who recognized me in the picture and sent them to this booth. I teared up to think how far all these New Yorkers had extended themselves to show such kindness to a girl from Oklahoma.

I was launching a sales trip across central Missouri on the morning of September 11, 2001, when life as we knew it changed. Ready to roll out of my motel room, I picked up the remote to turn off the TV as the CNBC business program announced a plane had flown into the World Trade Center. I knew work no longer mattered. I was going home. That normally five-hour trip back to Tulsa took all of ten hours because I felt too stunned and overwhelmed to drive safely at interstate highway speeds. Tearfully drifting down back roads, I realized the opportunity to promote Magshots to a higher level would have to wait. A humorous greeting card line was not appropriate during an unprecedented period of mourning. Over time, as the pain of September 11 subsided and laughter returned, our greeting card sales resumed.

A Voice in the Wind

MY ADA, OKLAHOMA, HIGH SCHOOL class held its fortieth reunion. It was a hot, humid Sunday evening in 2004, the festivities were over, and I was exhausted. For the last year, as class secretary, I had co-chaired our reunion committee with our class president, Schuyler Harold. The reunion kicked off Friday with a barbeque at the city park, followed by cheering for the mighty Cougars as they won a close game with the McAlester Buffalos.

Barbara Harris and Lynn Ramsay, my two best friends from kindergarten on, were among the one hundred and sixty in attendance. We talked into the wee hours of Saturday and Sunday mornings, the way we used to do at our slumber parties, and it affirmed the friendships we developed in spite of our mothers' idiosyncrasies.

As I was leaving town, high on memories of my youth, I decided to drive down Ada's Main Street, some twelve blocks long. I passed buildings that had meant so much to me. The old Dairy Queen, close to the college, now served as a Chinese takeout spot. The shade trees were gone, but the limestone gravel parking lot was just the same. At the end of this block, a Laundromat had replaced Tuck Drug. Catty-corner from Tuck's was Thena's house with her dance studio out back. The house had been converted to a small office building, and the studio was gone.

In the next block, the bakery and Greenspray Grocery had been replaced by franchises for tires and tax services. Further west, the old icehouse was gone, and the drive-in that took its place had been converted to a computer hardware store. The railroad tracks had been removed long ago. The Juliana Hotel was razed after I left town. Now there was a memorial park where it once stood. The First National Bank, where Clifford worked as a teller when I was born, was still at the intersection of Main and Broadway, One block west stood the McSwain Theater, where Frances played the piano for Thena McBride's early dance recitals.

"That felt good," I said to myself, so I decided to drive by 217 North Mississippi.

The street was no longer a narrow two-lane road. Now it was a five-lane thoroughfare that shrunk all the property on the west side of the block at the house where I lived my preschool years. Commercialism had eliminated the neighborhood ambiance. I parked my car around the corner on a side street, got out, and walked along the sidewalk in front of my first home.

The house had endured many conversions, but its core remained intact. It was a small house, maybe nine hundred square feet with two tiny bedrooms, a bath, a living room with a dining area, a kitchen, and a breakfast nook. It was built on a small lot behind my grandparents' home for Frances and Clifford before I was born. The house faced east, so we got the welcoming morning sun. It was set back from busy Mississippi Avenue. Only one of the pecan trees that had surrounded the house was still there. A detached garage stood on the west edge of the lot where hollyhocks once grew along its wall. An alley on the south side separated us from King's Grocery Store and the Blue Note Club that sometimes got too loud on Saturday nights.

I looked down at the cracked and dirty sidewalk.

"Where is it?" I said softly to myself as I walked slowly forward.

In a few paces, I found it, the sidewalk panel that had a large, jagged crack. It was still there. Whenever I saw that crack, though tempted, I never dared to step on it.

I had spent much of my lifetime reeling from the influence of my mother. I knew she cared, but she cared and controlled too much. She smothered me in fact. Someone would have thought she would have noticed what she did after my first divorce, after my anorexia nervosa, through my years of depression, during my years in therapy, or after my second divorce. But no. She was too unpredictable, critical, preoccupied, and psychically sick herself.

Ten years ago, shortly before Frances died, the pieces of my life that had been broken and scattered for so many years finally began to reassemble. Through persistence and hard work, I finally attained a life of contentment and satisfaction. As shadows fell on the house on 217 North Mississippi, where it all began, I got in my car to drive away. In the wind that whispered through the pecan leaves, I wondered if I heard Frances' voice? If so, I couldn't make out her words. But I believed she was saying that she was pleased with me. Yes, it was finally time for her to tell me so.

Postscript

I N THE LAST FEW YEARS, my new depression-free life has gained momentum. No longer on any medication, I am regularly logging at least six hours of uninterrupted sleep per night. I have more energy today than at any other time in my adult life. Pickleball, a game like tennis but with a paddle and Wiffle ball, is my new sport of choice and much easier on the knees.

I am finally all about seeking and embracing change and new experiences. My faith is strong, and I strive to live within His will, not mine. I see evidence that I am given no more than I can handle.

I suppose I could have called my book, *How I Survived Seven Therapists by Really, Really Trying.* Lyn and I recently talked about my therapeutic process. I am still in therapy. However, the sessions of support on a monthly basis are a far cry from the biweekly appointments of years ago. And, most importantly, the good news is that my dear friend Maggie was wrong. It is safe to say that I no longer consider therapy as a utility needed for the rest of my life.

Today, I enjoy spending time with my Oklahoma-grown grandchildren. I still look forward to a good perm.

Would your book club or writers group enjoy this book?

Additional copies are available for purchase at:
www.wheatmark.com or by calling 1-888-934-0888 Ext. 100.
Step on a Crack also available through many online retailers
or special order at your local bookstore.

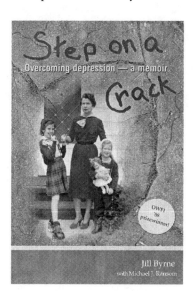

Step on a Crack
6x9, paperback,
252 pp, $19.95

Jill Byrne's inspirational memoir *Step on a Crack* shows how her indomitable spirit and sense of humor helped her survive childhood neglect, divorces, chronic and clinical depression, a psychotic episode, and a revolving door of therapists. Following her completion of the Hoffman Quadrinity Process, she removed the psychiatric gum from her shoe forever. In *Step on a Crack*, Jill tells of her recovery and offers hope to the millions in America who suffer from depression's anguish.

Printed in the United States
141704LV00001BB/2/P